Mediterranean Diet Cookbook for Beginners

2000+ Days of Super Easy & Delicious Recipes with a 30-Day Meal Plan – All Ready in 30 Minutes or Less for Busy People Who Want to Eat Healthy

Andrew Moore

Copyright © 2025 by Andrew Moore. All rights reserved.

No part of this book may be reproduced, distributed, or transmitted in any form or by any means without prior written permission from the publisher, except for brief quotations in reviews or critical articles.

Legal Disclaimer

The information in this book has been compiled from reliable sources and is presented with the author's best knowledge, belief, and expertise. However, the author accepts no liability for any errors or omissions.

TABLE OF CONTENTS

EDITOR'S LETTERS..................................6
How to Transition to the Mediterranean Diet......6
THE MEDITERRANEAN DIET – A TIMELESS PATH TO HEALTH AND LONGEVITY..................7
- Discovering the Mediterranean Diet: More Than Just a Way of Eating..........................7
- Why the Mediterranean Diet is One of the Healthiest in the World.......................7
- Building Your Mediterranean Pantry: Essential Ingredients for Health and Flavor.............8
- Exploring the Regional Contributions to the Mediterranean Diet.........................9
- Final Thoughts: A Journey to Health and Happiness..................................12

CHAPTER 2: 30-DAY MEAL PLAN...................13
CHAPTER 3: BREAKFASTS:........................16
Wholesome Whole Grain Breakfast Bowls........16
- Buckwheat Porridge with Walnuts and Figs..16
- Spelt Breakfast Bowl with Hazelnuts and Dark Chocolate............................16
- Brown Rice Pudding with Coconut Milk and Raisins...................................17
- Freekeh Breakfast Bowl with Dried Cherries and Tahini.................................17
- Polenta Breakfast Bowl with Ricotta and Balsamic Strawberries......................18
- Couscous Breakfast Bowl with Almond Butter and Sliced Apples..................18

CHAPTER 4: BREAKFASTS: Mediterranean-Style Egg Creations..................19
- Frittata with Roasted Red Peppers and Mozzarella...................................19
- Spanish Tortilla with Potatoes and Sweet Onions......................................19
- Baked Eggplant and Eggs with Sumac and Garlic.....................................20
- Scrambled Eggs with Smoked Salmon and Capers....................................20
- Egg and Ricotta Bake with Roasted Tomatoes and Thyme........................21
- Herb-Infused Omelet with Olives and Feta Cheese....................................21

CHAPTER 5: BREAKFASTS: Weekend Delights: Light and Refreshing Breakfasts........22
- Cinnamon-Spiced Persimmons with Ricotta. 22
- Savory Chickpea Flour Pancakes with Sun-Dried Tomatoes........................22
- Greek Yogurt and Olive Oil Cake..............23
- Pistachio and Lemon Buckwheat Pancakes. 23
- Ricotta and Honey Baked Pancakes.........24
- Mediterranean Casserole with Spinach and Sun-Dried Tomatoes......................24
- Baked Polenta with Figs and Walnuts.......25
- Zucchini and Feta Breakfast Frittata........25
- Savory Herb and Cheese Scones............26
- Sun-Dried Tomato and Goat Cheese Muffins..26
- Mediterranean Breakfast Pizza with Feta and Olives..................................27
- Spinach and Ricotta Quiche with Pine Nuts.. 27

CHAPTER 6: BREAKFASTS: Nutritious and Flavorful Smoothies......................28
- Chia and Blueberry Power Smoothie........28
- Lemon and Olive Oil Detox Smoothie.......28
- Cucumber and Mint Cooler Smoothie.......29
- Grape and Lavender Smoothie................29

CHAPTER 7: LUNCHES: Comforting Soups....30
and Stews..30
- Hearty Farro and Vegetable Soup with Olive Oil Drizzle................................30
- Italian Tomato and Basil Soup with Parmesan Crumbles.......................30
- Zucchini and Chickpea Soup with Thyme and Oregano...............................31
- Tuscan Kale and Cannellini Bean Soup with Parmesan....................................31
- Tomato and Eggplant Stew with Basil and Olive Oil....................................32
- Chickpea and Zucchini Stew with Fresh Mint..32
- Mediterranean Chicken and Eggplant Stew with Oregano..............................33
- Tomato and Garlic Beef Stew with Basil and Red Wine.................................33

CHAPTER 8: LUNCHES: Mediterranean........34
Grain Bowls: A Hearty Choice..................34

Buckwheat and Spinach Bowl with Caramelized Onions..................34
Wild Rice and Chickpea Bowl with Smoked Paprika Dressing..................34
Freekeh and Roasted Mushrooms Bowl with Tahini Sauce..................35
Millet and Roasted Cauliflower Bowl with Pine Nuts..................35
Wild Rice and Roasted Butternut Squash Bowl with Thyme..................36
Quinoa and Warm Chickpea Bowl with Lemon Zest and Olives..................36

CHAPTER 9: LUNCHES:..................37
Classic Mediterranean Pasta Dishes..................37

Macaroni with Greek Yogurt, Spinach, and Dill..................37
Tortellini with Roasted Peppers and Herbed Ricotta..................37
Pasta alla Norma with Roasted Eggplant and Ricotta Salata..................38
Spaghetti with Sun-Dried Tomatoes, Olives, and Basil Pesto..................38
Pasta with Butternut Squash, Sage, and Toasted Almonds..................39
Farfalle with Peas, Mint, and Parmesan Shavings..................39

CHAPTER 10: LUNCHES:..................40
Satisfying Meat-Based Lunches..................40

Moroccan Chicken with Green Olives and Preserved Lemon..................40
Garlic and Herb Marinated Lamb Chops with Grilled Peppers..................40
Mediterranean-Style Turkey Meatballs with Feta and Oregano..................41
Chicken Shawarma with Garlic Tahini Sauce 41
Spiced Ground Beef with Pine Nuts and Fresh Herbs..................42
One-Pan Chicken with Mushrooms and White Wine Sauce..................42
Greek-Style Grilled Chicken with Lemon and Dill Yogurt..................43
Quick Beef and Lentil Stir-Fry with Sumac 43
Chicken with Artichokes, Lemon, and Capers..................44
Balsamic Glazed Turkey Cutlets with Rosemary..................44

CHAPTER 11: SNACKS: Savory..................45
Mediterranean Appetizers and Dips..................45

Roasted Eggplant and Tahini Spread with Garlic..................45
Cucumber and Mint Yogurt Dip..................45
Zaatar-Spiced Chickpea and Tahini Dip Enjoy..................46
Muhammara (Roasted Red Pepper and Walnut Dip)..................46
Labneh with Fresh Herbs, Olive Oil, and Pomegranate Seeds..................47
Roasted Red Pepper and Yogurt Dip with Sumac..................47

CHAPTER 12: DESSERTS: Decadent Desserts with a Healthy Touch..................48

Mediterranean Apple and Almond Clafoutis.. 48
Orange and Almond Mediterranean Muffins 48
Mediterranean Olive Oil and Citrus Cake..49
Chocolate and Olive Oil Cake with Orange Glaze..................49
Raisin and Walnut Greek Easter Cookies (Koulourakia)..................50
Saffron and Pistachio Muffins with Yogurt. 50
Tahini and Maple Syrup Brownies..................51
Hazelnut and Cocoa Nib Cookies with Olive Oil..................51
Whole Wheat Banana and Honey Cake... 52
Almond and Apricot Bars..................52

CHAPTER 13: DESSERTS: Effortless..................53
No-Bake Mediterranean Sweets..................53

No-Bake Greek Yogurt Cheesecake with Honey and Walnuts..................53
Tahini and Dark Chocolate Truffles with Sesame Crunch..................53
Saffron and Almond Milk Panna Cotta with Cardamom..................54
No-Bake Chocolate and Olive Oil Tart with Sea Salt..................54
Pomegranate and Pistachio Ricotta Mousse 55
Rosewater and Fig Chia Pudding with Toasted Almonds..................55

CHAPTER 14: DINNER: Refreshing Mediterranean Salad Creations..................56

Roasted Eggplant and Lentil Salad with Basil and Balsamic..................56

Tomato and Mozzarella Caprese with Basil and Olive Oil......................................56
Cucumber and Mint Yogurt Salad with Sumac...57
Bulgur and Roasted Zucchini Salad with Lemon Dressing..57
Warm Roasted Beet and Goat Cheese Salad with Citrus Dressing........................58
Bulgur and Grilled Chicken Salad with Pomegranate Vinaigrette......................... 58
Arugula and Beef Salad with Sun-Dried Tomatoes and Parmesan........................... 59
Lentil and Roasted Chicken Salad with Garlic Yogurt Dressing............................... 59
Warm Farro and Grilled Lamb Salad with Lemon and Herbs......................................60
Chicken and Artichoke Salad with Basil and Pine Nuts..60

CHAPTER 15: DINNER: Easy One-Pan Dinners for Busy Evenings.................................. 61
Mediterranean One-Pan Balsamic Chicken with Roasted Tomatoes...............61
One-Skillet Moroccan Lamb with Olives and Peppers...61
Rosemary and Olive Oil Turkey with Roasted Cauliflower...............................62
One-Pan Mediterranean Chicken with Artichokes and Capers.............................62
Garlic and Cumin-Spiced Beef with Roasted Sweet Potatoes..................................63
Tomato and Basil One-Pan Turkey with Lentils..63

CHAPTER 16: DINNER: Coastal Favorites: Fish and Seafood Specialties.........................64
Shrimp Saganaki (Greek Shrimp in Tomato and Feta Sauce)...............................64
Roasted Mackerel with Olive and Sun-Dried Tomato Relish.................................. 64
Crispy Skillet Trout with Almond and Lemon Crust..65
Moroccan Spiced Grilled Tuna Steaks with Harissa Yogurt..65
Basil and Pine Nut Crusted Baked Halibut 66
Mediterranean Swordfish with Roasted Peppers and Capers................................. 66

CHAPTER 17: DINNER: Festive Family Feasts: Dishes for Special Gatherings..........................67
One-Pan Chicken Marbella with Olives and Capers..67
Slow-Braised Beef with Tomato and Red Wine Sauce..67
Tuscan White Bean and Sausage Stew with Fresh Thyme..68
Roasted Chicken with Sumac, Garlic, and Lemon Yogurt Sauce................................68
Spiced Lamb Meatballs in Warm Tomato and Cinnamon Sauce.................................69
One-Pan Beef and Roasted Vegetable Bake with Herbs... 69

CHAPTER 18: BONUSES...........................70
Effortless Mediterranean Meal Plans & Shopping Guides...................................70
Shopping List for 7-Day Meal Plan............70
Grocery Shopping List for 8-14 Day Meal Plan... 71
Grocery Shopping List for 15-21 Day Meal Plan... 73
Grocery Shopping List for 22-28 Day Meal Plan... 74

EDITOR'S LETTERS

Dear Reader,

Thank you for choosing this book. Whether you are just starting your journey to healthier eating or looking for fresh inspiration, I am delighted to guide you.

The Mediterranean diet is more than just food—it's a lifestyle that embraces fresh, wholesome ingredients, vibrant flavors, and balanced nutrition. It has been shown to support heart health, boost energy, and promote overall well-being. That's why I created this cookbook—to make healthy eating simple, quick, and accessible.

Inside, you'll find 2000+ days of easy and nutritious recipes inspired by the Mediterranean way of eating. To help you transition smoothly, I've also included a 30-day meal plan. From hearty breakfasts to flavorful dinners, each dish is designed to nourish your body and bring joy to your table.

This diet isn't about restriction—it's about enjoying food that makes you feel good while creating healthy, lasting habits. I hope this book inspires you to explore new flavors and embrace a balanced, fulfilling lifestyle.

With gratitude,

Andrew Moore

How to Transition to the Mediterranean Diet

Making the shift to Mediterranean-style eating doesn't have to be overwhelming. Start small by incorporating these **simple habits**:

✔ **Cook with Olive Oil** – Replace butter or processed oils with **extra virgin olive oil** for healthier cooking and better flavor.

✔ **Fill Half Your Plate with Vegetables** – Let fresh, seasonal vegetables become the star of your meals.

✔ **Eat Fish Twice a Week** – Opt for grilled or baked fish like **salmon, sardines, or mackerel**, which are high in omega-3s.

✔ **Choose Whole Grains** – Replace white bread and pasta with **fiber-rich options** like quinoa, whole wheat, or bulgur.

✔ **Snack Smart** – Keep nuts, seeds, and fresh fruit on hand for a **nutrient-packed, satisfying snack**.

✔ **Enjoy Meals with Family & Friends** – Make dining a social experience. Studies show that eating together reduces stress and enhances digestion.

THE MEDITERRANEAN DIET – A TIMELESS PATH TO HEALTH AND LONGEVITY

Discovering the Mediterranean Diet: More Than Just a Way of Eating

Welcome to the world of the **Mediterranean diet**, a time-honored way of eating that has nourished people for centuries. Unlike fleeting diet trends, the Mediterranean diet is rooted in tradition, culture, and science. It originated in the sun-kissed regions of Southern Europe, including Greece, Italy, and Spain, where people have long enjoyed vibrant, wholesome meals that promote health and longevity.

What sets the Mediterranean diet apart is its **focus on natural, nutrient-dense foods** that fuel the body while delighting the senses. It's not about restriction but about **balance and enjoyment**, featuring fresh vegetables, juicy fruits, whole grains, healthy fats, lean proteins, and flavorful herbs and spices. Meals are meant to be savored, shared, and celebrated—embracing food not just as sustenance but as a source of **connection, joy, and well-being**.

Why the Mediterranean Diet is One of the Healthiest in the World

Scientific research has extensively validated the **remarkable health benefits** of the Mediterranean diet. Studies show that people who follow this lifestyle experience:

✔ **A Healthier Heart** – The diet is rich in **monounsaturated fats** from olive oil and omega-3 fatty acids from fish, which help lower bad cholesterol and reduce the risk of heart disease. The **PREDIMED Study** in Spain (2013) found that the Mediterranean diet reduced the risk of cardiovascular events by **30%**.

✔ **Better Brain Function** – The antioxidants and healthy fats in this diet protect the brain from inflammation and cognitive decline, lowering the risk of **Alzheimer's disease** by up to **33%**, according to Greek neurological studies.

✔ **Balanced Blood Sugar Levels** – Whole grains, legumes, and fiber-rich vegetables help stabilize glucose levels, making this diet an excellent choice for people managing or preventing **type 2 diabetes**. A Spanish study (2014) found that it improved **blood sugar control by 27%**.

✔ **A Longer Life** – In regions like Ikaria, Greece, and Sardinia, Italy—known as "**Blue Zones**"—people commonly live into their **90s and beyond**, thanks to their adherence to the Mediterranean diet and an active, stress-free lifestyle.

✔ **Reduced Inflammation** – Chronic inflammation contributes to diseases like arthritis, obesity, and cancer. The Mediterranean diet is naturally **anti-inflammatory**, with its rich array of **fruits, vegetables, nuts, and omega-3s**. The **EPIC Study** in Europe (2013) found a **25% reduction in cancer risk** among those who followed this diet closely.

Building Your Mediterranean Pantry: Essential Ingredients for Health and Flavor

Extra Virgin Olive Oil – The foundation of Mediterranean cooking, rich in **heart-healthy monounsaturated fats and powerful antioxidants**. Use it in dressings, drizzled over vegetables, or for cooking.

Colorful Vegetables & Fruits – Think **tomatoes, leafy greens, bell peppers, berries, and citrus**. These provide vitamins, fiber, and disease-fighting antioxidants while adding natural sweetness and crunch to meals.

Whole Grains – Swap refined grains for **farro, quinoa, barley, and bulgur**, which are packed with fiber and nutrients that support digestion and **keep you feeling full longer**.

Lean Proteins – Mediterranean eating prioritizes **fish and seafood**, rich in omega-3s, while keeping red meat consumption low. Lean poultry, beans, and lentils are also excellent protein sources.

Nuts & Seeds – Almonds, walnuts, chia seeds, and flaxseeds are nutrient powerhouses, offering **healthy fats, protein, and fiber**. They make great snacks or toppings for yogurt and salads.

Herbs & Spices – Instead of relying on salt, Mediterranean cuisine uses **basil, oregano, rosemary, thyme, cumin, and cinnamon** to enhance flavors while delivering additional health benefits.

Exploring the Regional Contributions to the Mediterranean Diet

The **Mediterranean diet** is often regarded as a single way of eating, but in reality, it is a diverse culinary tradition influenced by the many cultures, climates, and histories of the countries surrounding the Mediterranean Sea. Each region brings unique flavors, ingredients, and techniques that have shaped this world-renowned diet into what it is today. From the **herb-rich dishes of Greece** to the **seafood specialties of Spain** and the **rustic, olive oil-infused meals of Italy**, the Mediterranean diet is a **mosaic of traditions** that highlight local agriculture and centuries-old cooking methods.

Greece: The Birthplace of Balanced Eating

Greece is often considered the **heart of the Mediterranean diet**, with its emphasis on fresh, seasonal ingredients and balanced meals. Greek cuisine revolves around **olive oil, legumes, whole grains, fresh vegetables, and moderate amounts of dairy and fish**. Popular dishes like **horiatiki (Greek salad), ladera (vegetables cooked in olive oil)**, and **lentil soup (fakes soupa)** showcase how Greeks prioritize plant-based meals, using **herbs like oregano, thyme, and dill** to enhance natural flavors.

One of Greece's greatest contributions to the Mediterranean diet is its **traditional approach to dairy**, particularly in the form of **fermented foods** such as **Greek yogurt and feta cheese**. Greek yogurt is an excellent source of **probiotics, protein, and calcium**, promoting gut health and digestion. Additionally, Greeks consume moderate amounts of **wild-caught fish**, such as sardines and anchovies, which are **rich in omega-3 fatty acids**, essential for heart and brain health.

Another Greek dietary tradition is **fasting**, particularly in the Greek Orthodox Church. Many Greeks follow periods of **plant-based fasting**, eliminating meat and dairy, which naturally aligns with modern health trends promoting plant-based diets. These fasting traditions, practiced for centuries, contribute to lower rates of **cardiovascular disease and metabolic disorders** among the Greek population.

Italy: The Art of Simplicity and Freshness

Italy is famous for its **vibrant, yet simple cuisine**, where quality ingredients take center stage. Unlike the misconception that Italian food revolves around **heavy pasta dishes**, traditional Italian meals are actually **light, fresh, and nutrient-dense**. The Italian Mediterranean diet focuses on **olive oil, tomatoes, garlic, whole grains, legumes, seafood, and a variety of seasonal vegetables**.

One of Italy's greatest contributions to the Mediterranean diet is the use of **whole grain and legume-based foods**, such as **farro, barley, chickpeas, and lentils**. These staples provide **fiber, plant-based protein, and essential vitamins**, promoting digestive health and sustained energy levels.

A major feature of Italian cuisine is its **"cucina povera"** tradition, meaning **"peasant food"**, which emphasizes **simple, affordable, and nutrient-dense meals**. Many classic Mediterranean dishes, such as **minestrone soup, panzanella (bread salad), and ribollita (Tuscan vegetable soup)**, originated from this tradition and are packed with **antioxidants, fiber, and healthy fats**.

Italians are also known for their **moderate wine consumption**, particularly **red wine**, which contains **resveratrol**, an antioxidant linked to **heart health and longevity**. The Italian practice of **slow eating, sharing meals with family, and prioritizing whole foods over processed alternatives** is a fundamental principle of the Mediterranea

Spain: The Seafood and Superfood Powerhouse

Spain's contribution to the Mediterranean diet is its **incredible variety of seafood, legumes, and antioxidant-rich spices**. Spanish cuisine is deeply rooted in the use of **heart-healthy olive oil, fresh seafood, nuts, and colorful vegetables**, which together provide an ideal balance of **healthy fats, protein, and fiber**.

One of Spain's most famous Mediterranean staples is **gazpacho**, a cold tomato-based soup that is **packed with lycopene**, a powerful antioxidant known for its **anti-inflammatory and heart-protective** benefits. Another well-known Spanish dish, **paella**, is a **protein-rich, nutrient-dense meal** that combines seafood, whole grains (such as brown rice or bomba rice), and **spices like saffron and paprika**, which have anti-inflammatory properties.

Spain is also one of the largest producers of **almonds, walnuts, and hazelnuts**, which are essential to the Mediterranean diet. These nuts provide **plant-based omega-3s, protein, and vitamin E**, all of which contribute to **brain function, heart health, and anti-aging benefits**.

Spanish meals are often **social occasions**, following the **"tapas" tradition**, where people gather to enjoy **small, nutrient-dense plates** of olives, grilled vegetables, nuts, and seafood. This **shared eating culture** encourages mindful eating, reduces stress, and fosters **a strong sense of community**, which plays a key role in overall well-being.

Morocco: The Fusion of Spices and Superfoods

Though not always included in Mediterranean diet discussions, **North African countries like Morocco play a vital role in shaping Mediterranean cuisine**. Moroccan food combines Mediterranean staples with nutrient-dense North African spices and cooking methods.

One of Morocco's key contributions is **couscous**, a **fiber-rich whole grain** made from durum wheat that provides a steady release of energy and **supports digestive health**. Moroccan cuisine also makes extensive use of **chickpeas, lentils, and fava beans**, which are rich in **plant-based protein, iron, and fiber**.

Spices such as **turmeric, cumin, coriander, and cinnamon** are heavily used in Moroccan dishes like **tagine (slow-cooked stew)**. These spices not only add incredible flavor but also possess **anti-inflammatory and immune-boosting properties**.

Another standout Moroccan ingredient is **argan oil**, which, like olive oil, is rich in **healthy fats and antioxidants**. While primarily known for its skin benefits, **culinary-grade argan oil** is used in cooking and has been shown to **lower cholesterol and improve heart health**.

Turkey and the Eastern Mediterranean: A Blend of Tradition and Nutrition

The Eastern Mediterranean, particularly **Turkey, Lebanon, and Israel**, offers some of the most diverse and nutritious dishes within the Mediterranean diet. The foundation of this cuisine includes **whole grains, legumes, nuts, fresh herbs, and fermented dairy products**.

One of the region's greatest contributions is **hummus**, made from chickpeas, tahini (sesame seed paste), olive oil, garlic, and lemon juice. This dish is packed with **plant-based protein, fiber, and heart-healthy fats**, making it a staple for those following a Mediterranean-style diet.

Fermented dairy, particularly **labneh (strained yogurt)** and **kefir**, is widely consumed in this region. These foods are rich in **probiotics**, which **support gut health, boost immunity, and improve digestion**.

Eastern Mediterranean cuisine also places a strong emphasis on **herbs like mint, parsley, and sumac**, which not only enhance flavors but also provide **anti-inflammatory and digestive benefits**.

11

Final Thoughts: A Journey to Health and Happiness

The Mediterranean diet is more than just a meal plan—it's a **lifelong commitment to health, balance, and joy**. By adopting this way of eating, you're not only nourishing your body with some of the healthiest foods on the planet, but you're also embracing a sustainable and fulfilling lifestyle.

Whether your goal is **better heart health, increased energy, weight management, or simply enjoying delicious, wholesome meals**, the Mediterranean diet is a proven path to **long-term well-being**.

So, as you embark on this journey, remember: **it's not about strict rules, but about enjoying real food, shared experiences, and the simple pleasures of life.**

Welcome to a way of eating that's as joyful as it is healthy!

CHAPTER 2: 30-DAY MEAL PLAN

Day	Breakfast	Lunch	Snack	Dinner
Day 1	Buckwheat Porridge with Walnuts and Figs - p.16	Hearty Farro and Vegetable Soup with Olive Oil - p.30	Roasted Eggplant and Tahini Spread with Garlic - p.45	Mediterranean One-Pan Balsamic Chicken - p.61
Day 2	Scrambled Eggs with Smoked Salmon and Capers - p.20	Wild Rice and Roasted Butternut Squash Bowl - p.36	Muhammara (Roasted Red Pepper and Walnut Dip) - p.46	Shrimp Saganaki (Greek Shrimp in Tomato and Feta) - p.64
Day 3	Chia and Blueberry Power Smoothie - p.28	Macaroni with Greek Yogurt, Spinach, and Dill - p.37	No-Bake Greek Yogurt Cheesecake with Honey - p.53	One-Skillet Moroccan Lamb with Olives - p.61
Day 4	Ricotta and Honey Baked Pancakes - p.24	Tomato and Eggplant Stew with Basil and Olive Oil - p.32	Saffron and Pistachio Muffins with Yogurt - p.50	Crispy Skillet Trout with Almond and Lemon - p.65
Day 5	Freekeh Breakfast Bowl with Dried Cherries - p.17	Mediterranean Chicken and Eggplant Stew - p.33	Pomegranate and Pistachio Ricotta Mousse - p.55	Garlic and Cumin-Spiced Beef with Sweet Potatoes - p.63
Day 6	Frittata with Roasted Red Peppers and Mozzarella - p.19	Quinoa and Warm Chickpea Bowl with Lemon Zest - p.36	Labneh with Herbs, Olive Oil, and Pomegranate - p.47	Moroccan Spiced Grilled Tuna Steaks - p.65
Day 7	Pistachio and Lemon Buckwheat Pancakes - p.23	Garlic and Herb Marinated Lamb Chops - p.40	Zaatar-Spiced Chickpea and Tahini Dip - p.46	One-Pan Chicken Marbella with Olives - p.67
Day 8	Egg and Ricotta Bake with Roasted Tomatoes - p.21	Spaghetti with Sun-Dried Tomatoes and Basil Pesto - p.38	Tahini and Dark Chocolate Truffles - p.53	Balsamic Glazed Turkey Cutlets with Rosemary - p.44
Day 9	Cinnamon-Spiced Persimmons with Ricotta - p.22	Moroccan Chicken with Green Olives - p.40	Orange and Almond Mediterranean Muffins - p.48	Roasted Mackerel with Olive and Tomato Relish - p.64
Day 10	Spelt Breakfast Bowl with Hazelnuts and Chocolate - p.16	Italian Tomato and Basil Soup with Parmesan - p.30	Rosewater and Fig Chia Pudding with Almonds - p.55	Slow-Braised Beef with Tomato and Red Wine - p.67
Day 11	Baked Eggplant and Eggs with Sumac - p.20	Tuscan Kale and Cannellini Bean Soup - p.31	Hazelnut and Cocoa Nib Cookies - p.51	Mediterranean Swordfish with Roasted Peppers - p.66
Day 12	Cucumber and Mint Cooler Smoothie - p.29	Zucchini and Chickpea Soup with Thyme - p.31	Almond and Apricot Bars - p.52	Roasted Chicken with Sumac and Lemon Yogurt - p.68
Day 13	Sun-Dried Tomato and Goat Cheese Muffins - p.26	Tortellini with Roasted Peppers and Ricotta - p.37	Whole Wheat Banana and Honey Cake - p.52	Spiced Lamb Meatballs with Tomato Sauce - p.69
Day 14	Herb-Infused Omelet with Olives and Feta - p.21	Pasta with Butternut Squash and Sage - p.39	No-Bake Chocolate and Olive Oil Tart - p.54	One-Pan Beef and Roasted Vegetable Bake - p.69
Day 15	Greek Yogurt and Olive Oil Cake - p.23	Balsamic Glazed Turkey Cutlets with Rosemary - p.44	Raisin and Walnut Greek Easter Cookies - p.50	Tuscan White Bean and Sausage Stew - p.68

Day	Breakfast	Lunch	Snack	Dinner
Day 16	Zucchini and Feta Breakfast Frittata - p.25	Chickpea and Zucchini Stew with Fresh Mint - p.32	Roasted Red Pepper and Yogurt Dip - p.47	Warm Farro and Grilled Lamb Salad - p.60
Day 17	Polenta Breakfast Bowl with Ricotta and Strawberries - p.18	Buckwheat and Spinach Bowl - p.34	Pomegranate and Pistachio Ricotta Mousse - p.55	Mediterranean Chicken with Artichokes - p.62
Day 18	Savory Chickpea Flour Pancakes with Tomatoes - p.22	Wild Rice and Chickpea Bowl - p.34	Orange and Almond Mediterranean Muffins - p.48	One-Pan Mediterranean Chicken with Capers - p.62
Day 19	Lemon and Olive Oil Detox Smoothie - p.28	Freekeh and Roasted Mushrooms Bowl - p.35	Muhammara (Red Pepper and Walnut Dip) - p.46	Tomato and Basil One-Pan Turkey with Lentils - p.63
Day 20	Spanish Tortilla with Potatoes and Onions - p.19	Millet and Roasted Cauliflower Bowl - p.35	No-Bake Chocolate and Olive Oil Tart - p.54	Garlic and Cumin-Spiced Beef - p.63
Day 21	Couscous Bowl with Almond Butter and Apples - p.18	Farfalle with Peas and Mint - p.39	Zaatar-Spiced Chickpea and Tahini Dip - p.46	One-Pan Chicken Marbella with Olives - p.67
Day 22	Mediterranean Breakfast Pizza with Feta - p.27	One-Pan Chicken with Mushrooms - p.42	Tahini and Maple Syrup Brownies - p.51	Grilled Tuna Steaks with Harissa Yogurt - p.65
Day 23	Spinach and Ricotta Quiche with Pine Nuts - p.27	Greek-Style Grilled Chicken with Lemon Yogurt - p.43	Saffron and Almond Milk Panna Cotta - p.54	Basil and Pine Nut Crusted Halibut - p.66
Day 24	Baked Polenta with Figs and Walnuts - p.25	Chicken with Artichokes and Capers - p.44	Roasted Red Pepper and Yogurt Dip - p.47	Slow-Braised Beef with Tomato and Red Wine - p.67
Day 25	Savory Herb and Cheese Scones - p.26	Quick Beef and Lentil Stir-Fry with Sumac - p.43	Pomegranate and Pistachio Ricotta Mousse - p.55	Moroccan Spiced Lamb Shoulder - p.69
Day 26	Brown Rice Pudding with Coconut Milk - p.17	Tomato and Garlic Beef Stew with Basil - p.33	No-Bake Chocolate and Olive Oil Tart - p.54	One-Pan Beef and Roasted Vegetable Bake - p.69
Day 27	Tomato and Basil Bruschetta with Poached Eggs - p.20	Mediterranean Turkey Meatballs - p.41	Almond and Apricot Bars - p.52	Roasted Chicken with Sumac and Yogurt Sauce - p.68
Day 28	Pistachio and Lemon Buckwheat Pancakes - p.23	Spiced Ground Beef with Pine Nuts - p.42	Labneh with Fresh Herbs and Pomegranate - p.47	Mediterranean Swordfish with Roasted Peppers - p.66
Day 29	Savory Chickpea Flour Pancakes - p.22	One-Pan Mediterranean Chicken - p.62	No-Bake Greek Yogurt Cheesecake - p.53	Tuscan White Bean and Sausage Stew - p.68
Day 30	Chia and Blueberry Power Smoothie - p.28	Garlic and Cumin-Spiced Beef - p.63	Hazelnut and Cocoa Nib Cookies - p.51	One-Skillet Moroccan Lamb - p.61

Note: This 30-day meal plan is a flexible guide to explore Mediterranean flavors. Nutritional values are approximate and can vary based on portions and ingredients. Emphasizing fresh vegetables, lean proteins, and healthy fats, this plan encourages you to adjust portions and ingredients to fit your needs. Enjoy the vibrant, adaptable nature of the Mediterranean diet on your wellness journey!

15

CHAPTER 3: BREAKFASTS:
Wholesome Whole Grain Breakfast Bowls

Buckwheat Porridge with Walnuts and Figs

Prep: 5 minutes | Cook: 15 minutes | Serves: 1

Ingredients:

- 1/4 cup raw buckwheat groats (50g)
- 3/4 cup whole milk or Greek yogurt mixed with 1/4 cup water
- 1 tbsp walnuts, chopped (15g)
- 1 small fig, chopped (40g) 1/2 tsp ground cinnamon
- 1 tsp honey
- Pinch of salt

Instructions:

1. Rinse buckwheat under cold water.
2. In a saucepan, combine buckwheat, milk (or yogurt-water mix), cinnamon, and salt. Bring to a boil, then simmer for 10–15 minutes, stirring occasionally.
3. Stir in honey, transfer to a bowl, and top with chopped walnuts and figs..

Nutritional Facts (Per Serving): Calories: 370 | Carbs: 30g | Protein: 13g | Fat: 14g | Fiber: 8g | Sodium: 760mg | Sugars: 9g

Spelt Breakfast Bowl with Hazelnuts and Dark Chocolate

Prep: 5 minutes | Cook: 20 minutes | Serves: 1

Ingredients:

- 1/4 cup spelt flakes (40g)
- 3/4 cup whole milk or water
- 1 tbsp pistachios, chopped (15g) Pinch of salt
- 1 small date, chopped (10g)
- 1/2 tsp ground cinnamon
- 1/2 tsp vanilla extract

Instructions:

1. Rinse spelt and cook with milk (or water), cinnamon, and salt over medium heat, stirring occasionally.
2. Cook until tender, checking for doneness after 15 minutes (may take up to 25 minutes).
3. Stir in vanilla, transfer to a bowl, and top with chopped pistachios and dates.

Nutritional Facts (Per Serving): Calories: 380 | Carbs: 29g | Protein: 18g | Fat: 15g | Fiber: 7g | Sodium: 770mg | Sugars: 10g

Brown Rice Pudding with Coconut Milk and Raisins

Prep: 5 minutes | Cook: 25 minutes | Serves: 1

Ingredients:

- 1/2 cup cooked brown rice (100g)
- 1/2 cup unsweetened coconut milk (120ml)
- 1 tbsp raisins (15g)
- 1 tsp honey
- 1/4 tsp vanilla extract
- 1/2 tsp ground cinnamon
- Pinch of salt

Instructions:

1. Combine cooked rice, coconut milk, raisins (or chosen substitute), cinnamon, and salt in a saucepan.
2. Place the saucepan over medium heat and bring the mixture to a gentle boil, stirring occasionally.
3. Reduce the heat to low and let it simmer for 10–15 minutes, stirring occasionally, until the pudding thickens to your desired consistency.
4. Remove the saucepan from heat and stir in vanilla extract and honey.
5. Transfer the pudding to a bowl, serve warm, and garnish with cinnamon if desired.

Nutritional Facts (Per Serving): Calories: 380 | Carbs: 28g | Protein: 17g | Fat: 15g | Fiber: 7g | Sodium: 780mg | Sugars: 12g

Freekeh Breakfast Bowl with Dried Cherries and Tahini

Prep: 5 minutes | Cook: 20 minutes | Serves: 1

Ingredients:

- 1/4 cup cooked freekeh (50g)
- 3/4 cup whole milk or Greek yogurt mixed with 1/4 cup water
- 1 tbsp dried apricots, chopped (15g)
- 1 tsp tahini (5g)
- 1/2 tsp ground cardamom
- 1 tsp honey
- Pinch of salt

Instructions:

1. In a saucepan, combine cooked freekeh, milk (or yogurt-water mix), cardamom, and salt, stirring to mix.
2. Heat over medium heat, stirring occasionally, until it starts to bubble gently.
3. Reduce heat to low and simmer for 10–15 minutes, stirring occasionally, until creamy.
4. Stir in honey and transfer to a bowl.
5. Top with chopped dried apricots and drizzle with tahini.

Nutritional Facts (Per Serving): Calories: 360 | Carbs: 29g | Protein: 18g | Fat: 14g | Fiber: 8g | Sodium: 50mg | Sugars: 10g

Polenta Breakfast Bowl with Ricotta and Balsamic Strawberries

Prep: 5 minutes | Cook: 10 minutes | Serves: 1

Ingredients:

- 1/4 cup quick-cooking polenta (40g)
- 3/4 cup unsweetened almond milk (180ml)
- 1/4 cup ricotta cheese (60g)
- 1/4 cup fresh strawberries, chopped (40g)
- 1 tsp balsamic vinegar
- 1 tsp honey
- Pinch of salt

Instructions:

1. In a small saucepan, whisk together polenta, almond milk, and a pinch of salt.
2. Cook over medium heat, stirring frequently, for about 5 minutes, until the polenta thickens and becomes creamy.
3. While the polenta is cooking, toss the finely chopped strawberries with balsamic vinegar and honey in a small bowl. Set aside to marinate.
4. Once the polenta is ready, transfer it to a serving bowl. Top with ricotta cheese and the balsamic strawberries.

Nutritional Facts (Per Serving): Calories: 370 | Carbs: 29g | Protein: 17g | Fat: 14g | Fiber: 6g | Sodium: 780mg | Sugars: 10g

Couscous Breakfast Bowl with Almond Butter and Sliced Apples

Prep: 5 minutes | Cook: 5 minutes | Serves: 1

Ingredients:

- 1/4 cup whole wheat couscous (40g)
- 1/4 cup hot water (60ml)
- 1 tbsp tahini (15g)
- 1 tsp honey
- 1/4 small apple, thinly sliced (40g)
- 1/4 tsp ground cinnamon
- Pinch of salt

Instructions:

1. In a small bowl, combine couscous and hot water.
2. Cover the bowl tightly with a plate or plastic wrap and let it sit for 5 minutes.
3. Remove the cover and fluff the couscous with a fork.
4. Add tahini, honey, ground cinnamon, and a pinch of salt. Mix thoroughly.
5. Top with thinly sliced apples before serving.

Nutritional Facts (Per Serving): Calories: 360 | Carbs: 28g | Protein: 18g | Fat: 15g | Fiber: 7g | Sodium: 770mg | Sugars: 9g

CHAPTER 4: BREAKFASTS:
Mediterranean-Style Egg Creations

Frittata with Roasted Red Peppers and Mozzarella

Prep: 10 minutes | Cook: 20 minutes | Serves: 1

Ingredients:

- 3 large eggs
- 1/4 cup roasted red peppers, chopped (40g)
- 1/4 cup shredded mozzarella cheese (30g)
- 2 tbsp whole milk (30ml)
- 1 tbsp olive oil (15ml)
- 1/4 tsp salt
- 1/4 tsp black pepper

Instructions:

1. Preheat oven to 375°F (190°C). Whisk eggs, milk, salt, and pepper.
2. Heat olive oil in an oven-safe skillet, cook red peppers for 2 minutes.
3. Pour the egg mixture into the skillet, cook for 3-4 minutes until edges set.
4. Sprinkle mozzarella on top and bake in the oven for 10 minutes until fully set.
5. Let cool for 5 minutes before serving.

Nutritional Facts (Per Serving): Calories: 370 | Carbs: 6g | Protein: 23g | Fat: 15g | Fiber: 5g | Sodium: 780mg | Sugars: 7g

Spanish Tortilla with Potatoes and Sweet Onions

Prep: 10 minutes | Cook: 30 minutes | Serves: 1

Ingredients:

- 2 large eggs
- 1/2 cup diced potatoes (75g)
- 1/4 cup sweet onions, thinly sliced (40g)
- 2 tbsp olive oil (30ml)
- 1/4 tsp salt
- 1/4 tsp black pepper

Instructions:

1. Sauté potatoes and onions in 1 tbsp olive oil in an 8-10-inch skillet over medium heat for 10-12 minutes.
2. Whisk eggs with salt and pepper. Stir in the cooked potatoes and onions.
3. Heat the remaining oil in the skillet, pour in the egg mixture, and cook for 5 minutes. Flip the tortilla and cook for another 5 minutes until set.

Nutritional Facts (Per Serving): Calories: 390 | Carbs: 25g | Protein: 18g | Fat: 14g | Fiber: 6g | Sodium: 770mg | Sugars: 8g

Baked Eggplant and Eggs with Sumac and Garlic

Prep: 10 minutes | Cook: 25 minutes | Serves: 1

Ingredients:

- 1 small eggplant, sliced (150g)
- 2 large eggs
- 1 tbsp olive oil (15ml)
- 1/2 tsp sumac
- 1 garlic clove, minced (3g)
- 1/4 tsp salt
- 1/4 tsp black pepper

Instructions:

1. Preheat the oven to 375°F (190°C) and line a baking sheet with parchment or grease lightly.
2. Arrange eggplant slices on the baking sheet. Brush with olive oil and sprinkle with garlic, salt, and black pepper.
3. Bake the eggplant for 15 minutes, or until it becomes tender and lightly golden.
4. Remove from the oven. Crack the eggs directly over the baked eggplant slices, keeping the yolks intact.
5. Sprinkle the sumac evenly over the top.
6. Return to the oven and bake for 8–10 minutes, or until the eggs are cooked to your preference.

Nutritional Facts (Per Serving): Calories: 370 | Carbs: 14g | Protein: 17g | Fat: 15g | Fiber: 6g | Sodium: 780mg | Sugars: 8g

Scrambled Eggs with Smoked Salmon and Capers

Prep: 5 minutes | Cook: 10 minutes | Serves: 1

Ingredients:

- 3 large eggs
- 2 oz smoked salmon, chopped (60g)
- 1 tbsp capers (15g)
- 1 tbsp whole milk (15ml)
- 1 tsp olive oil (5ml)
- 1/4 tsp salt
- 1/4 tsp black pepper

Instructions:

1. Whisk eggs, whole milk, salt, and pepper in a bowl.
2. Heat olive oil in a skillet over medium heat.
3. Pour in the egg mixture and gently stir while cooking.
4. When eggs are almost set, fold in smoked salmon and capers.
5. Serve warm with optional extra capers for garnish.

Nutritional Facts (Per Serving): Calories: 390 | Carbs: 2g | Protein: 25g | Fat: 15g | Fiber: 5g | Sodium: 800mg | Sugars: 7g

Egg and Ricotta Bake with Roasted Tomatoes and Thyme

Prep: 10 minutes | Cook: 25 minutes | Serves: 1

Ingredients:

- 2 large eggs
- 1/4 cup ricotta cheese (60g)
- 1/2 cup cherry tomatoes, halved (75g)
- 1 tsp olive oil (5ml)
- 1/4 tsp dried thyme
- 1/4 tsp salt
- 1/4 tsp black pepper

Instructions:

1. Preheat the oven to 375°F (190°C) and grease a small baking dish with olive oil.
2. In a mixing bowl, whisk together the eggs, ricotta cheese, salt, and black pepper until the mixture is smooth and creamy. Set aside.
3. Arrange the halved cherry tomatoes in a single layer of the greased baking dish. Drizzle with olive oil and sprinkle evenly with dried thyme for added flavor.
4. Pour the egg and ricotta mixture over the tomatoes.
5. Bake for 20–25 minutes, or until the eggs are set and lightly golden.

Nutritional Facts (Per Serving): Calories: 360 | Carbs: 7g | Protein: 20g | Fat: 15g | Fiber: 5g | Sodium: 780mg | Sugars: 8g

Herb-Infused Omelet with Olives and Feta Cheese

Prep: 5 minutes | Cook: 10 minutes | Serves: 1

Ingredients:

- 3 large eggs
- 2 tbsp crumbled feta cheese (30g)
- 1 tbsp black olives, sliced (15g)
- 1 tsp olive oil (5ml)
- 1/4 tsp dried oregano
- 1/4 tsp salt
- 1/4 tsp black pepper

Instructions:

1. In a bowl, whisk eggs, oregano, salt, and pepper.
2. Heat olive oil in a nonstick skillet over medium heat.
3. Pour in the egg mixture and let cook for 2–3 minutes.
4. Sprinkle feta cheese and olives on one half.
5. Fold the omelet and cook for another 1–2 minutes.
6. Serve warm.

Nutritional Facts (Per Serving): Calories: 370 | Carbs: 4g | Protein: 22g | Fat: 15g | Fiber: 5g | Sodium: 790mg | Sugars: 7g

CHAPTER 5: BREAKFASTS: Weekend Delights: Light and Refreshing Breakfasts

Cinnamon-Spiced Persimmons with Ricotta

Prep: 5 minutes | Cook: 5 minutes | Serves: 1

Ingredients:

- 1 ripe persimmon, sliced (150g)
- 1/4 cup ricotta cheese (60g)
- 1/4 tsp ground cinnamon
- 1/2 tsp olive oil (2.5ml)
- 1 tsp honey (7g)

Instructions:

1. Heat a nonstick skillet over medium heat with olive oil.
2. Add persimmon slices in a single layer, sprinkle with cinnamon, and cook for 2–3 minutes per side until softened.
3. Transfer to a plate, top with ricotta, drizzle with honey, and serve warm.

Nutritional Facts (Per Serving): Calories: 370 | Carbs: 27g | Protein: 17g | Fat: 14g | Fiber: 6g | Sodium: 770mg | Sugars: 12g

Savory Chickpea Flour Pancakes with Sun-Dried Tomatoes

Prep: 10 minutes | Cook: 15 minutes | Serves: 1

Ingredients:

- 1/2 cup chickpea flour (60g)
- 1/4 cup water (60ml)
- 2 tbsp sun-dried tomatoes, chopped (15g)
- 1 tsp olive oil (5ml)
- 1 tbsp fresh parsley, chopped (5g)
- 1/4 tsp salt
- 1/4 tsp black pepper

Instructions:

1. Whisk chickpea flour, water, salt, pepper, sun-dried tomatoes, and parsley until smooth.
2. Heat half the olive oil in a skillet on medium. Pour in half the batter and cook 4 minutes per side.
3. Grease the skillet with the remaining oil and cook the rest of the batter.
4. Garnish with parsley, if desired, and serve warm.

Nutritional Facts (Per Serving): Calories: 390 | Carbs: 24g | Protein: 19g | Fat: 14g | Fiber: 7g | Sodium: 780mg | Sugars: 8g

Greek Yogurt and Olive Oil Cake

Prep: 10 minutes | Cook: 25 minutes | Serves: 1

Ingredients:

- 1/2 cup plain Greek yogurt (120g)
- 2 large eggs
- 1/4 cup olive oil (60ml)
- 1/2 cup whole wheat flour (60g)
- 1 tbsp honey
- 1 tsp baking powder
- 1/4 tsp salt
- 1/2 tsp lemon zest

Instructions:

1. Preheat oven to 350°F (175°C) and line a small loaf pan with parchment paper.
2. In a bowl, whisk yogurt, eggs, olive oil, and lemon zest until smooth.
3. In another bowl, mix whole wheat flour, baking powder, and salt.
4. Gradually fold dry ingredients into wet mixture.
5. Pour batter into prepared pan and smooth the top.
6. Bake 25–30 minutes until a toothpick comes out clean. Cool before slicing.

Nutritional Facts (Per Serving): Calories: 380 | Carbs: 9g | Protein: 19g | Fat: 15g | Fiber: 6g | Sodium: 780mg | Sugars: 8g

Pistachio and Lemon Buckwheat Pancakes

Prep: 10 minutes | Cook: 15 minutes | Serves: 1

Ingredients:

- 1/4 cup buckwheat flour (40g)
- 1/4 cup whole grain flour (30g)
- 1/4 cup milk (60ml)
- 1 large egg
- 2 tbsp pistachios, chopped (15g)
- 1 tsp lemon zest
- 1 tbsp olive oil (15ml)
- 1 tsp honey
- 1/2 tsp baking powder
- Pinch of salt

Instructions:

1. Toast pistachios in a dry skillet for 1–2 minutes for enhanced flavor.
2. Whisk buckwheat flour, whole grain flour, baking powder, sweetener, and salt.
3. Mix milk, egg, lemon zest, and 1 tsp olive oil, then combine with dry ingredients until smooth.
4. Heat a skillet, brush with oil, and cook 2 tbsp of batter per pancake for 2–3 minutes per side.
5. Repeat with remaining batter and serve with toasted pistachios.

Nutritional Facts (Per Serving): Calories: 390 | Carbs: 20g | Protein: 20g | Fat: 15g | Fiber: 7g | Sodium: 780mg | Sugars: 9g

Ricotta and Honey Baked Pancakes

Prep: 10 minutes | Cook: 20 minutes | Serves: 1

Ingredients:

- 1/4 cup ricotta cheese (60g)
- 1 large egg
- 2 tbsp whole grain flour (15g)
- 1 tbsp honey (15g)
- 1/4 tsp baking powder
- 1/4 tsp ground cinnamon
- 1/2 tsp olive oil (2.5ml)

Instructions:

1. Preheat the oven to 375°F (190°C) and grease a small baking dish with olive oil.
2. In a medium-sized mixing bowl, combine the ricotta cheese, egg, whole grain flour honey, baking powder, and ground cinnamon. Whisk until the batter is smooth and all ingredients are evenly incorporated.
3. Pour the batter into the greased baking dish. Use a spatula to smooth the surface so it bakes evenly.
4. Place the dish in the preheated oven and bake for 18–20 minutes, or until the top turns golden and the pancake is set in the center.
5. Let cool slightly before serving. Optionally, drizzle with a bit of honey for extra sweetness.

Nutritional Facts (Per Serving): Calories: 380 | Carbs: 14g | Protein: 18g | Fat: 15g | Fiber: 6g | Sodium: 770mg | Sugars: 10g

Mediterranean Casserole with Spinach and Sun-Dried Tomatoes

Prep: 10 minutes | Cook: 25 minutes | Serves: 1

Ingredients:

- 2 large eggs
- 1/4 cup crumbled feta cheese (60g)
- 1 cup fresh spinach, chopped (40g)
- 1 tbsp olive oil (15ml)
- 1/4 tsp dried oregano
- 2 tbsp sun-dried tomatoes, chopped (15g)
- 1/4 tsp salt
- 1/4 tsp black pepper

Instructions:

1. Preheat the oven to 375°F (190°C) and grease a small casserole dish with olive oil.
2. In a bowl, whisk eggs with salt, pepper, and oregano.
3. Layer spinach, sun-dried tomatoes, and feta cheese in the casserole dish.
4. Pour the egg mixture over the top, ensuring it evenly coats the ingredients.
5. Bake for 20–25 minutes, or until the eggs are set and the top is golden.
6. Let cool slightly before serving.

Nutritional Facts (Per Serving): Calories: 390 | Carbs: 10g | Protein: 20g | Fat: 15g | Fiber: 7g | Sodium: 780mg | Sugars: 9g

Baked Polenta with Figs and Walnuts

Prep: 10 minutes | Cook: 25 minutes | Serves: 1

Ingredients:

- 1/2 cup cooked polenta (120g)
- 2 fresh figs, sliced (100g)
- 2 tbsp chopped walnuts (15g)
- 1 tbsp honey (15g)
- 1 tsp olive oil (5ml)
- 1/4 tsp ground cinnamon

Instructions:

1. Preheat the oven to 375°F (190°C) and grease a small baking dish with olive oil.
2. Spread the cooked polenta evenly in the dish and smooth the surface. Arrange fig slices on top and sprinkle with walnuts.
3. Drizzle honey over the figs and walnuts, then lightly dust with cinnamon.
4. Bake for 20–25 minutes until the edges of the polenta are golden and the figs are tender.
5. Remove from the oven, let cool for a few minutes, and serve warm with the dish's juices.

Nutritional Facts (Per Serving): Calories: 370 | Carbs: 28g | Protein: 17g | Fat: 15g | Fiber: 7g | Sodium: 770mg | Sugars: 12g

Zucchini and Feta Breakfast Frittata

Prep: 10 minutes | Cook: 20 minutes | Serves: 1

Ingredients:

- 2 large eggs
- 1/2 cup zucchini, grated (50g)
- 1/4 cup crumbled feta cheese (60g)
- 1 tbsp olive oil (15ml)
- 1/4 tsp dried oregano
- 1/4 tsp salt
- 1/4 tsp black pepper

Instructions:

1. Preheat the oven to 375°F (190°C). Heat olive oil in an oven-safe skillet over medium heat.
2. Grate the zucchini and squeeze out excess moisture using a towel and sauté for 2–3 minutes until softened and slightly golden. Remove from heat and let cool slightly.
3. In a bowl, whisk eggs, salt, pepper, and oregano. Stir in crumbled feta cheese and the cooked zucchini.
4. Pour the mixture into the skillet, spreading it evenly. Transfer the skillet to the oven.
5. Bake for 15–20 minutes until the frittata is set and lightly golden. Test with a knife; it should come out clean.

Nutritional Facts (Per Serving): Calories: 380 | Carbs: 6g | Protein: 20g | Fat: 15g | Fiber: 5g | Sodium: 780mg | Sugars: 8g

Savory Herb and Cheese Scones

Prep: 10 minutes | Cook: 20 minutes | Serves: 1

Ingredients:

- 1/2 cup whole grain flour (60g)
- 1/4 cup shredded cheddar cheese (30g)
- 1 large egg
- 1 tbsp butter, melted (15g)
- 1/2 tsp baking powder
- 1/4 tsp dried oregano
- 1/4 tsp dried thyme
- 1/4 tsp salt
- 1/4 tsp black pepper

Instructions:

1. Preheat the oven to 375°F (190°C) and line a baking sheet with parchment paper.
2. Mix whole grain flour, cheddar cheese, baking powder, oregano, thyme, salt, and pepper in a bowl.
3. Whisk egg and melted butter in a small bowl, then combine with the dry ingredients to form a dough.
4. Shape the dough into a disc on the baking sheet, cut into 4 wedges, and slightly separate them.
5. Bake for 18–20 minutes until golden brown and firm. Let cool for 5 minutes before serving.

Nutritional Facts (Per Serving): Calories: 370 | Carbs: 9g | Protein: 18g | Fat: 15g | Fiber: 6g | Sodium: 780mg | Sugars: 7g

Sun-Dried Tomato and Goat Cheese Muffins

Prep: 10 minutes | Cook: 25 minutes | Serves: 1

Ingredients:

- 1/2 cup whole wheat flour (60g) 1/4 cup crumbled goat cheese (30g)
- 2 tbsp chopped sun-dried tomatoes (15g)
- 1 large egg
- 1 tbsp olive oil (15ml)
- 1/2 tsp baking powder
- 1/4 tsp dried basil
- 1/4 tsp salt
- 1/4 tsp black pepper

Instructions:

1. Preheat oven to 375°F (190°C). Grease a muffin tin or line with paper cups.
2. In a bowl, mix whole wheat flour, baking powder, basil, salt, pepper, goat cheese, and sun-dried tomatoes.
3. Whisk the egg and olive oil in a separate bowl, then combine with the dry ingredients to form a thick batter.
4. Divide batter into 2 muffin cups, filling each about three-quarters full.
5. Bake for 20–25 minutes, or until golden and a toothpick inserted in the center comes out clean.

Nutritional Facts (Per Serving): Calories: 380 | Carbs: 10g | Protein: 19g | Fat: 15g | Fiber: 7g | Sodium: 790mg | Sugars: 9g

Mediterranean Breakfast Pizza with Feta and Olives

Prep: 10 minutes | Cook: 15 minutes | Serves: 1

Ingredients:

- 1 whole-wheat tortilla (50g)
- 2 large eggs
- 1/4 cup crumbled feta cheese (30g)
- 2 tbsp black olives, sliced (15g)
- 2 tbsp chopped sun-dried tomatoes (15g)
- 1 tsp olive oil (5ml)
- 1/4 tsp dried oregano

Instructions:

1. Preheat the oven to 400°F (200°C) and place the tortilla on a baking sheet.
2. Brush the tortilla lightly with olive oil and sprinkle with dried oregano.
3. Crack the eggs directly onto the tortilla, spacing them apart.
4. Top with crumbled feta, olives, and sun-dried tomatoes.
5. Bake for 12–15 minutes, or until the eggs are set and the edges of the tortilla are crispy.
6. Slice and serve warm.

Nutritional Facts (Per Serving): Calories: 380 | Carbs: 14g | Protein: 20g | Fat: 15g | Fiber: 6g | Sodium: 780mg | Sugars: 8g

Spinach and Ricotta Quiche with Pine Nuts

Prep: 10 minutes | Cook: 25 minutes | Serves: 1

Ingredients:

- 2 large eggs
- 1/4 cup ricotta cheese (60g)
- 1 cup fresh spinach, chopped (40g)
- 1 tbsp pine nuts, toasted (10g)
- 1/4 cup whole grain flour (30g)
- 1 tbsp olive oil (15ml)
- 1/2 tsp baking powder
- 1/4 tsp salt
- 1/4 tsp black pepper

Instructions:

1. Preheat the oven to 375°F (190°C) and grease a quiche dish with olive oil.
2. Sauté spinach for 2–3 minutes until wilted and let cool. Toast pine nuts, then cool before using.
3. Whisk eggs, ricotta, salt, and pepper. Stir in spinach, pine nuts, and whole grain flour mixed with baking powder.
4. Pour into the prepared dish and bake for 20–25 minutes until golden and set. Let cool slightly before serving.

Nutritional Facts (Per Serving): Calories: 390 | Carbs: 10g | Protein: 21g | Fat: 15g | Fiber: 7g | Sodium: 790mg | Sugars: 9g

CHAPTER 6: BREAKFASTS: Nutritious and Flavorful Smoothies

Chia and Blueberry Power Smoothie

Prep: 5 minutes | Cook: 0 minutes | Serves: 1

Ingredients:

- 1/4 cup fresh blueberries (40g)
- 1/2 cup plain Greek yogurt (120g)
- 1 tbsp chia seeds (15g)
- 1/2 cup water1 tsp honey

Instructions:

1. Combine blueberries, Greek yogurt, chia seeds, almond milk, and honey in a blender.
2. Blend on high speed for 30–60 seconds until smooth and creamy.
3. Let the mixture sit for 5 minutes to allow the chia seeds to swell.
4. Blend again briefly, then pour into a glass. Adjust the consistency with more almond milk if desired.

Nutritional Facts (Per Serving): Calories: 370 | Carbs: 22g | Protein: 20g | Fat: 14g | Fiber: 7g | Sodium: 780mg | Sugars: 12g

Lemon and Olive Oil Detox Smoothie

Prep: 5 minutes | Cook: 0 minutes | Serves: 1

Ingredients:

- 1/2 lemon, juiced (30ml)
- 1/2 cucumber, chopped (50g)
- 1/2 tsp fresh ginger, grated (2g)
- 1 tbsp extra virgin olive oil (15ml)
- 1/2 cup cold water (120ml)

Instructions:

1. Add lemon juice, cucumber, ginger, olive oil, and cold water to a blender.
2. Blend on high for 30–60 seconds, or until the mixture is smooth and well combined.
3. For a smoother texture, strain the smoothie through a fine mesh sieve.
4. Pour the smoothie into a glass and serve immediately.

Nutritional Facts (Per Serving): Calories: 360 | Carbs: 10g | Protein: 16g | Fat: 14g | Fiber: 5g | Sodium: 780mg | Sugars: 8g

Cucumber and Mint Cooler Smoothie

Prep: 5 minutes | Cook: 0 minutes | Serves: 1

Ingredients:

- 1/2 cucumber, peeled and chopped (50g)
- 2 tbsp fresh mint leaves (6g)
- 1/2 cup cold water (120ml)
- 1 tsp lime juice (5ml)
- 1 tsp honey (7g)
- 1/4 cup plain Greek yogurt (60g)

Instructions:

1. Place the cucumber, fresh mint leaves, cold water, lime juice, honey, and plain Greek yogurt into a blender.
2. Blend on high speed for 30–60 seconds, or until the mixture becomes creamy and smooth.
3. Check the consistency. If it's too thick, add a splash of water and blend again to reach your desired texture.
4. Taste the smoothie and adjust the sweetness by adding more honey or balance the tartness with an extra squeeze of lime juice, if needed.

Nutritional Facts (Per Serving): Calories: 400 | Sugars: 5g | Fat: 15g | Carbs: 25g | Protein: 16g | Fiber: 7g | Sodium: 370mg

Grape and Lavender Smoothie

Prep: 5 minutes | Cook: 20 minutes | Serves: 1

Ingredients:

- 1/2 cup red grapes (75g)
- 1/2 cup plain Greek yogurt (120g)
- 1/2 tsp edible lavender (1g)
- 1/4 cup cold water (60ml)
- 1 tsp honey (7g)

Instructions:

1. Place the red grapes, Greek yogurt, edible lavender, cold water, and honey into a blender.
2. Blend on high speed for 30–60 seconds, or until the mixture becomes creamy and smooth. If you prefer a silkier texture, strain the smoothie through a fine-mesh sieve to remove any grape skins or seeds.
3. Taste the smoothie and adjust the sweetness by adding more honey if needed. Blend briefly to incorporate.
4. Pour the smoothie into a serving glass, ensuring it stays chilled.
5. Garnish with a few grapes, a light sprinkle of lavender, or both for a decorative finish.

Nutritional Facts (Per Serving): Calories: 400 | Sugars: 4g | Fat: 14g | Carbs: 9g | Protein: 18g | Fiber: 6g | Sodium: 350mg

CHAPTER 7: LUNCHES: Comforting Soups and Stews

Hearty Farro and Vegetable Soup with Olive Oil Drizzle

Prep: 10 minutes | Cook: 20 minutes | Serves: 1

Ingredients:

- 1/4 cup farro (50g)
- 2 cups vegetable broth (475ml)
- 1/2 cup diced zucchini (80g)
- 1/4 cup diced carrot (40g)
- 1/4 cup chopped celery (40g)
- 2 tbsp diced onion (30g)
- 1 garlic clove, minced
- 1 tbsp olive oil (15ml)
- 1 tsp dried Italian herbs (2g)
- Salt and pepper to taste

Instructions:

1. Cook farro in 1 cup broth for 10-12 minutes.
2. Sauté onion, garlic, carrot, and celery in olive oil for 5 minutes.
3. Add zucchini, broth, and herbs; simmer 10 minutes.
4. Mix in farro, season, and serve.

Nutritional Facts (Per Serving): Calories: 450 | Carbs: 30g | Protein: 22g | Fat: 20g | Fiber: 9g | Sodium: 550mg | Sugars: 5g

Italian Tomato and Basil Soup with Parmesan Crumbles

Prep: 10 minutes | Cook: 20 minutes | Serves: 1

Ingredients:

- 1 cup canned diced tomatoes (240g)
- 1 cup vegetable broth (240ml)
- 2 tbsp chopped fresh basil (10g)
- 1 garlic clove, minced
- 1/4 cup grated Parmesan cheese (30g)
- 1 tbsp olive oil (15ml)
- 1/4 tsp crushed red pepper flakes (1g)
- Salt and pepper to taste

Instructions:

1. Heat olive oil in a pot, sauté garlic and red pepper flakes for 1 minute. Add tomatoes and broth, simmer for 15 minutes.
2. Cool the soup for 5 minutes, then blend until smooth. Stir in basil, season with salt and pepper, and serve with Parmesan crumbles.

Nutritional Facts (Per Serving): Calories: 470 | Carbs: 25g | Protein: 24g | Fat: 21g | Fiber: 8g | Sodium: 580mg | Sugars: 6g

Zucchini and Chickpea Soup with Thyme and Oregano

Prep: 10 minutes | **Cook:** 20 minutes | **Serves:** 1

Ingredients:

- 1/2 cup canned chickpeas, drained and rinsed (90g)
- 1 cup diced zucchini (150g)
- 1 1/2 cups vegetable broth (360ml)
- 1 garlic clove, minced
- 1 tbsp olive oil (15ml)
- 1/2 tsp dried thyme (1g)
- 1/2 tsp dried oregano (1g)
- Salt and pepper to taste

Instructions:

1. Heat olive oil in a pot over medium heat.
2. Add the minced garlic to the pot and sauté to 1 minute.
3. Stir in the diced zucchini, dried thyme, and oregano. Cook for 5 minutes.
4. Stir in chickpeas and vegetable broth. Simmer for 15 minutes.
5. Reduce the heat to low and cook for 10-12 minutes.
6. Blend half the soup for a creamy texture, leaving some chickpeas whole.
7. Season with salt and pepper.

Nutritional Facts (Per Serving): Calories: 480 | Carbs: 28g | Protein: 21g | Fat: 20g | Fiber: 9g | Sodium: 560mg | Sugars: 3g

Tuscan Kale and Cannellini Bean Soup with Parmesan

Prep: 10 minutes | **Cook:** 20 minutes | **Serves:** 1

Ingredients:

- 1 cup chopped Tuscan kale (60g)
- 1/2 cup canned cannellini beans, drained and rinsed (90g)
- 1 1/2 cups vegetable broth (360ml)
- 1 garlic clove, minced
- 1 tbsp olive oil (15ml)
- 1 tbsp grated Parmesan cheese (5g)
- 1/4 tsp crushed red pepper flakes (1g)
- Salt and pepper to taste

Instructions:

1. Heat olive oil in a pot over medium heat.
2. Add the minced garlic and red pepper flakes to the pot, stirring frequently, and cook to 1 minute, until fragrant.
3. Add kale and cook for 5 minutes until wilted.
4. Stir in cannellini beans and vegetable broth. Bring the soup to a gentle simmer and cook for 10-12 minutes.
5. Season with salt and pepper. Serve hot with Parmesan sprinkled on top.

Nutritional Facts (Per Serving): Calories: 460 | Carbs: 27g | Protein: 22g | Fat: 18g | Fiber: 9g | Sodium: 580mg | Sugars: 4g

Tomato and Eggplant Stew with Basil and Olive Oil

Prep: 10 minutes | Cook: 20 minutes | Serves: 1

Ingredients:

- 1 cup diced eggplant (150g)
- 1 cup chopped tomatoes (150g)
- 1 tbsp olive oil (15ml)
- 1 clove garlic, minced
- 1/4 cup chopped fresh basil (10g)
- 1/4 tsp sea salt (1g)
- 1/4 tsp ground black pepper (1g)

Instructions:

1. Heat olive oil in a medium skillet over medium heat.
2. Add the minced garlic and sauté for 1 minute until fragrant, being careful not to burn it.
3. Stir in the diced eggplant and cook for 5-7 minutes, stirring occasionally, until it softens and starts to brown.
4. Stir in tomatoes, salt, and pepper, and simmer for 10-12 minutes until the mixture thickens.
5. Remove the skillet from heat, sprinkle the stew with fresh basil, and stir gently.

Nutritional Facts (Per Serving): Calories: 470 | Carbs: 22g | Protein: 22g | Fat: 21g | Fiber: 10g | Sodium: 550mg | Sugars: 6g

Chickpea and Zucchini Stew with Fresh Mint

Prep: 10 minutes | Cook: 20 minutes | Serves: 1

Ingredients:

- 1/2 cup cooked chickpeas (85g)
- 1 cup diced zucchini (150g)
- 1 tbsp olive oil (15ml)
- 1 clove garlic, minced
- 1/4 cup chopped fresh mint (10g)
- 1/4 tsp sea salt (1g)
- 1/4 tsp ground black pepper (1g)

Instructions:

1. Heat olive oil in a medium pot over medium heat.
2. Add garlic and sauté until golden, about 1 min.
3. Stir in the diced zucchini and cook for 5-7 minutes, stirring occasionally, until it softens slightly and begins to brown.
4. Add the cooked chickpeas to the pot and season with sea salt and black pepper. Stir well to combine.
5. Reduce the heat to low and let the stew simmer for 10 minutes, stirring occasionally, until the zucchini is tender and the flavors meld together.
6. Remove from heat, sprinkle with fresh mint, and serve warm.

Nutritional Facts (Per Serving): Calories: 480 | Carbs: 27g | Protein: 23g | Fat: 19g | Fiber: 9g | Sodium: 500mg | Sugars: 4g

Mediterranean Chicken and Eggplant Stew with Oregano

Prep: 10 minutes | Cook: 20 minutes | Serves: 1

Ingredients:

- 4 oz diced chicken breast (115g)
- 1 cup diced eggplant (150g)
- 1/2 cup chopped tomatoes (120g)
- 1 tbsp olive oil (15ml)
- 1 clove garlic, minced
- 1/2 tsp dried oregano (1g)
- 1/4 tsp sea salt (1g)
- 1/4 tsp black pepper (1g)

Instructions:

1. Heat olive oil in a medium skillet over medium heat. Add chicken and cook for 4-5 minutes until lightly browned.
2. Add garlic and sauté for 1 minute until fragrant.
3. Stir in eggplant and cook for 5 minutes, stirring occasionally.
4. Add tomatoes, oregano, salt, and pepper.
5. Cover and simmer on low heat for 10 minutes until the chicken is fully cooked and the eggplant is tender.
6. Serve warm, garnished with a sprinkle of oregano if desired.

Nutritional Facts (Per Serving): Calories: 480 | Carbs: 18g | Protein: 24g | Fat: 20g | Fiber: 8g | Sodium: 500mg | Sugars: 6g

Tomato and Garlic Beef Stew with Basil and Red Wine

Prep: 10 minutes | Cook: 20 minutes | Serves: 1

Ingredients:

- 4 oz lean beef cubes (115g)
- 1/2 cup chopped tomatoes (120g)
- 1/4 cup dry red wine (60ml)
- 1 tbsp olive oil (15ml)
- 1 clove garlic, minced
- 1/4 cup chopped fresh basil (10g)
- 1/4 tsp sea salt (1g)
- 1/4 tsp black pepper (1g)

Instructions:

1. Heat olive oil in a medium pot over medium-high heat.
2. Add the beef cubes and cook for 3-4 minutes, stirring occasionally, until they are browned on all sides.
3. Add the minced garlic and sauté for 1 minute, stirring frequently to prevent burning.
4. Stir in tomatoes, red wine, salt, and pepper. Reduce heat to low and simmer for 12-15 minutes, stirring occasionally, until beef is tender.
5. Remove from heat and stir in fresh basil. Let the flavors meld for 1-2 minutes before serving.

Nutritional Facts (Per Serving): Calories: 500 | Carbs: 10g | Protein: 25g | Fat: 22g | Fiber: 8g | Sodium: 450mg | Sugars: 3g

CHAPTER 8: LUNCHES: Mediterranean Grain Bowls: A Hearty Choice

Buckwheat and Spinach Bowl with Caramelized Onions

Prep: 10 minutes | Cook: 20 minutes | Serves: 1

Ingredients:

- 1/2 cup cooked buckwheat (85g)
- 1/2 medium onion, thinly sliced (50g)
- 1 cup fresh spinach (30g)
- 1 tbsp olive oil (15ml)
- 1/4 tsp sea salt (1g)
- 1/4 tsp black pepper (1g)

Instructions:

1. Heat a skillet over medium heat and add olive oil.
2. Add the sliced onion and cook for 8-10 minutes.
3. Warm the buckwheat in a pot or microwave.
4. Add spinach to the skillet with the onions and cook for 1-2 minutes until wilted.
5. Combine buckwheat, spinach, and onions in a bowl. Season with salt and black pepper.

Nutritional Facts (Per Serving): Calories: 485 | Carbs: 29g | Protein: 15g | Fat: 12g | Fiber: 7g | Sodium: 520 mg | Sugars: 9g

Wild Rice and Chickpea Bowl with Smoked Paprika Dressing

Prep: 10 minutes | Cook: 20 minutes | Serves: 1

Ingredients:

- 1/2 cup cooked wild rice (85g)
- 1/2 cup cooked chickpeas (85g)
- 1 cup arugula (30g)
- 1 tbsp olive oil (15ml)
- 1/2 tsp smoked paprika (2g)
- 1 tsp lemon juice (5ml)
- 1/4 tsp sea salt (1g)
- 1/4 tsp black pepper (1g)

Instructions:

1. Whisk olive oil, smoked paprika, lemon juice, salt, and pepper in a small bowl.
2. Warm wild rice and chickpeas in a skillet or microwave.
3. In a bowl, combine arugula, warm rice, and chickpeas. Drizzle with dressing and serve.

Nutritional Facts (Per Serving): Calories: 490 | Carbs: 30g | Protein: 23g | Fat: 20g | Fiber: 9g | Sodium: 450mg | Sugars: 3g

Freekeh and Roasted Mushrooms Bowl with Tahini Sauce

Prep: 10 minutes | Cook: 20 minutes | Serves: 1

Ingredients:

- 1/2 cup cooked freekeh (85g)
- 1 cup sliced mushrooms (100g)
- 1 tbsp olive oil (15ml)
- 1 tbsp tahini (15ml)
- 1 tsp lemon juice (5ml)
- 1/4 tsp sea salt (1g)
- 1/4 tsp black pepper (1g)
- 1/2 cup arugula (15g)

Instructions:

1. Preheat oven to 400°F (200°C).
2. Toss mushrooms with olive oil, salt, and pepper. Spread them on a baking sheet in a single layer and roast for 15 minutes, flipping halfway through.
3. In a small bowl, whisk together tahini, lemon juice, and 1 tbsp water in a small bowl until smooth and creamy. Adjust the consistency with a bit more water if needed.
4. Layer freekeh, roasted mushrooms, and arugula in a serving bowl.
5. Drizzle with tahini sauce and serve warm.

Nutritional Facts (Per Serving): Calories: 490 | Carbs: 28g | Protein: 22g | Fat: 20g | Fiber: 9g | Sodium: 500mg | Sugars: 3g

Millet and Roasted Cauliflower Bowl with Pine Nuts

Prep: 10 minutes | Cook: 20 minutes | Serves: 1

Ingredients:

- 1/2 cup cooked millet (85g)
- 1 cup cauliflower florets (100g)
- 1 tbsp olive oil (15ml)
- 1 tbsp pine nuts (10g)
- 1 tsp lemon juice (5ml)
- 1/4 tsp smoked paprika (1g)
- 1/4 tsp sea salt (1g)
- 1/4 tsp black pepper (1g)

Instructions:

1. Preheat the oven to 400°F (200°C).
2. Toss the cauliflower florets with olive oil, smoked paprika, salt, and pepper. Roast for 15 minutes.
3. Toast pine nuts in a dry skillet over medium heat for 1-2 minutes until golden.
4. Warm the cooked millet in a skillet or microwave.
5. In a serving bowl, layer the millet, roasted cauliflower, and toasted pine nuts.
6. Drizzle with lemon juice and toss lightly to combine.

Nutritional Facts (Per Serving): Calories: 480 | Carbs: 27g | Protein: 21g | Fat: 21g | Fiber: 8g | Sodium: 450mg | Sugars: 2g

Wild Rice and Roasted Butternut Squash Bowl with Thyme

Prep: 10 minutes | Cook: 20 minutes | Serves: 1

Ingredients:

- 1/2 cup cooked wild rice (85g)
- 1 cup diced butternut squash (150g)
- 1 tbsp olive oil (15ml)
- 1/4 tsp dried thyme (1g)
- 1/4 tsp sea salt (1g)
- 1/4 tsp black pepper (1g)
- 1/2 cup arugula (15g)

Instructions:

1. Preheat the oven to 400°F (200°C).
2. Place the diced butternut squash in a bowl and toss with olive oil, dried thyme, sea salt, and black pepper.
3. Spread the squash evenly on a baking sheet and roast for 15 minutes, flipping halfway through to ensure even cooking.
4. While the squash roasts, warm the cooked wild rice in a skillet over low heat or in the microwave.
5. In a serving bowl, layer the warm wild rice, roasted butternut squash, and fresh arugula.
6. Toss lightly to combine, garnish with extra thyme if desired, and serve warm.

Nutritional Facts (Per Serving): Calories: 480 | Carbs: 27g | Protein: 21g | Fat: 20g | Fiber: 9g | Sodium: 500mg | Sugars: 4g

Quinoa and Warm Chickpea Bowl with Lemon Zest and Olives

Prep: 10 minutes | Cook: 20 minutes | Serves: 1

Ingredients:

- 1/2 cup cooked quinoa (85g)
- 1/2 cup cooked chickpeas (85g)
- 1 tbsp olive oil (15ml)
- 1 tsp lemon zest (2g)
- 1 tbsp sliced olives (15g)
- 1/4 tsp sea salt (1g)
- 1/4 tsp black pepper (1g)
- 1/2 cup baby spinach (15g)

Instructions:

1. Heat olive oil in a skillet over medium heat. Add chickpeas and cook for 3-4 minutes until warm.
2. Stir in the lemon zest, sliced olives, sea salt, and black pepper. Cook for another 1-2 minutes to allow the flavors to blend.
3. Warm the quinoa in a separate skillet or microwave.
4. In a serving bowl, layer the quinoa at the base, followed by baby spinach, and then the warm chickpea mixture on top.
5. Toss gently to combine, ensuring the flavors are evenly distributed.

Nutritional Facts (Per Serving): Calories: 490 | Carbs: 28g | Protein: 23g | Fat: 21g | Fiber: 9g | Sodium: 450mg | Sugars: 3g

CHAPTER 9: LUNCHES:
Classic Mediterranean Pasta Dishes

Macaroni with Greek Yogurt, Spinach, and Dill

Prep: 10 minutes | Cook: 20 minutes | Serves: 1

Ingredients:

- 1/2 cup cooked whole wheat macaroni (85g)
- 1/2 cup fresh spinach (15g)
- 1/4 cup plain Greek yogurt (60g)
- 1 tbsp olive oil (15ml)
- 1 tsp chopped fresh dill (2g)
- 1 clove garlic, minced
- 1/4 tsp sea salt (1g)
- 1/4 tsp black pepper (1g)

Instructions:

1. Cook macaroni as directed, drain, and set aside.
2. Sauté garlic in olive oil over medium heat for 1 minute. Add spinach and cook until wilted, 1-2 minutes.
3. Mix Greek yogurt, dill, salt, and pepper in a bowl. Toss with macaroni and spinach.

Nutritional Facts (Per Serving): Calories: 480 | Carbs: 29g | Protein: 23g | Fat: 20g | Fiber: 8g | Sodium: 450mg | Sugars: 3g

Tortellini with Roasted Peppers and Herbed Ricotta

Prep: 10 minutes | Cook: 20 minutes | Serves: 1

Ingredients:

- 1/2 cup cooked tortellini (85g)
- 1/4 cup roasted red peppers, sliced (60g)
- 1/4 cup ricotta cheese (60g)
- 1 tsp chopped fresh basil (2g)
- 1 tsp chopped fresh parsley (2g)
- 1 tbsp olive oil (15ml)
- 1/4 tsp sea salt (1g)
- 1/4 tsp black pepper (1g)

Instructions:

1. Cook tortellini as directed, drain, and set aside.
2. Sauté roasted peppers in olive oil for 1-2 minutes until warm. Mix ricotta, basil, parsley, salt, and pepper in a bowl.
3. Toss tortellini with peppers, then fold in herbed ricotta. Serve warm, garnished with basil.

Nutritional Facts (Per Serving): Calories: 490 | Carbs: 27g | Protein: 22g | Fat: 21g | Fiber: 8g | Sodium: 500mg | Sugars: 4g

Pasta alla Norma with Roasted Eggplant and Ricotta Salata

Prep: 10 minutes | Cook: 20 minutes | Serves: 1

Ingredients:

- 1/2 cup cooked pasta (85g)
- 1 cup diced eggplant (150g)
- 1 tbsp olive oil (15ml)
- 1/2 cup tomato sauce (120g)
- 2 tbsp grated ricotta salata (15g)
- 1 clove garlic, minced
- 1/4 tsp sea salt (1g)
- 1/4 tsp black pepper (1g)
- Fresh basil leaves for garnish

Instructions:

1. Preheat oven to 400°F (200°C).
2. Toss eggplant with olive oil, salt, and pepper. Roast on a baking sheet for 15 minutes, flipping halfway through.
3. Cook pasta according to package instructions, drain, and set aside.
4. Heat tomato sauce in a skillet over medium heat. Add roasted eggplant and stir to combine.
5. Toss pasta with the sauce and transfer to a serving bowl.
6. Top with ricotta salata, garnish with fresh basil.

Nutritional Facts (Per Serving): Calories: 490 | Carbs: 28g | Protein: 22g | Fat: 20g | Fiber: 9g | Sodium: 500mg | Sugars: 4g

Spaghetti with Sun-Dried Tomatoes, Olives, and Basil Pesto

Prep: 10 minutes | Cook: 20 minutes | Serves: 1

Ingredients:

- 1/2 cup cooked spaghetti (85g)
- 2 tbsp chopped sun-dried tomatoes (15g)
- 1 tbsp sliced olives (15g)
- 1 tbsp basil pesto (15g)
- 1 tbsp olive oil (15ml)
- 1/4 tsp sea salt (1g)
- 1/4 tsp black pepper (1g)
- Fresh basil leaves for garnish

Instructions:

1. Cook spaghetti according to package instructions, drain, and set aside.
2. Heat olive oil in a skillet over medium heat.
3. Add the chopped sun-dried tomatoes and sliced olives, and sauté for 1-2 minutes until they are warmed through and slightly fragrant.
4. Toss the cooked spaghetti with basil pesto, then add the tomato-olive mixture. Mix well to combine.
5. Serve the spaghetti warm in a bowl, garnished with fresh basil leaves for a burst of color and flavor.

Nutritional Facts (Per Serving): Calories: 480 | Carbs: 27g | Protein: 21g | Fat: 21g | Fiber: 8g | Sodium: 450mg | Sugars: 3g

Pasta with Butternut Squash, Sage, and Toasted Almonds

Prep: 10 minutes | Cook: 20 minutes | Serves: 1

Ingredients:

- 1/2 cup cooked pasta (85g)
- 1 cup diced butternut squash (150g)
- 1 tbsp olive oil (15ml)
- 1 tsp chopped fresh sage (2g)
- 1 tbsp sliced almonds (10g)
- 1 clove garlic, minced
- 1/4 tsp sea salt (1g)
- 1/4 tsp black pepper (1g)

Instructions:

1. Preheat oven to 400°F (200°C).
2. Toss butternut squash with olive oil, salt, and pepper. Roast on a baking sheet for 15 minutes, flipping halfway through.
3. Toast almonds in a dry skillet over medium heat for 1-2 minutes until golden.
4. Cook pasta according to package instructions, drain, and set aside.
5. Heat a skillet over medium heat. Sauté garlic and sage in a little olive oil for 1 minute until fragrant.
6. Combine pasta, roasted squash, and sage mixture. Top with toasted almonds and serve warm.

Nutritional Facts (Per Serving): Calories: 480 | Carbs: 28g | Protein: 22g | Fat: 20g | Fiber: 9g | Sodium: 500mg | Sugars: 4g

Farfalle with Peas, Mint, and Parmesan Shavings

Prep: 10 minutes | Cook: 20 minutes | Serves: 1

Ingredients:

- 1/2 cup cooked farfalle (85g)
- 1/2 cup cooked peas (75g)
- 1 tbsp olive oil (15ml)
- 1 tsp chopped fresh mint (2g)
- 2 tbsp shaved Parmesan cheese (15g)
- 1 clove garlic, minced
- 1/4 tsp sea salt (1g)
- 1/4 tsp black pepper (1g)

Instructions:

1. Cook farfalle according to package instructions, drain, and set aside.
2. Heat olive oil in a skillet over medium heat. Add garlic and sauté for 1 minute until fragrant.
3. Stir in the cooked peas and sauté for an additional 1-2 minutes until warmed through. Remove the skillet from heat.
4. In a mixing bowl, combine the cooked farfalle, peas, and garlic mixture. Add chopped mint and toss gently to mix.
5. Transfer to a serving plate, top with Parmesan shavings, and season with salt and pepper to taste.

Nutritional Facts (Per Serving): Calories: 490 | Carbs: 27g | Protein: 23g | Fat: 21g | Fiber: 8g | Sodium: 450mg | Sugars: 3g

CHAPTER 10: LUNCHES:
Satisfying Meat-Based Lunches

Moroccan Chicken with Green Olives and Preserved Lemon

Prep: 10 minutes | Cook: 20 minutes | Serves: 1

Ingredients:

- 4 oz chicken breast, diced (115g)
- 1/4 cup green olives, sliced (35g)
- 1 tbsp preserved lemon, chopped (15g)
- 1 tbsp olive oil (15ml)
- 1/2 tsp ground cumin (1g)
- 1/4 tsp ground turmeric (1g)
- 1/4 tsp sea salt (1g)
- 1/4 tsp black pepper (1g)
- 1/4 cup chicken broth (60ml)
- Fresh cilantro for garnish

Instructions:

1. Heat olive oil, cook chicken 4-5 minutes.
2. Add spices, olives, lemon, and broth. Simmer for 10-12 minutes until chicken is cooked through and sauce thickens.
3. Garnish with cilantro and serve.

Nutritional Facts (Per Serving): Calories: 500 | Carbs: 2g | Protein: 25g | Fat: 23g | Fiber: 1g | Sodium: 450mg | Sugars: 0g

Garlic and Herb Marinated Lamb Chops with Grilled Peppers

Prep: 10 minutes | Cook: 20 minutes | Serves: 1

Ingredients:

- 2 lamb chops (120g)
- 1 red bell pepper, sliced (120g)
- 1 tbsp olive oil (15ml)
- 1 clove garlic, minced
- 1 tsp chopped fresh rosemary (2g)
- 1 tsp chopped fresh thyme (2g)
- 1/4 tsp sea salt (1g)
- 1/4 tsp black pepper (1g)

Instructions:

1. In a small bowl, mix olive oil, garlic, rosemary, thyme, salt, and pepper. Rub the mixture over the lamb chops and let marinate for 10 minutes.
2. Heat a grill pan and grill lamb chops 4 minutes per side.
3. In the same pan, grill bell pepper slices for 4-5 minutes until slightly charred and tender.

Nutritional Facts (Per Serving): Calories: 490 | Carbs: 9g | Protein: 25g | Fat: 22g | Fiber: 8g | Sodium: 450mg | Sugars: 4g

Mediterranean-Style Turkey Meatballs with Feta and Oregano

Prep: 10 minutes | Cook: 20 minutes | Serves: 1

Ingredients:

- 4 oz ground turkey (115g)
- 2 tbsp crumbled feta cheese (30g)
- 1 tsp chopped fresh oregano (2g)
- 1 clove garlic, minced
- 1 tbsp olive oil (15ml)
- 1/4 tsp sea salt (1g)
- 1/4 tsp black pepper (1g)
- 1/4 cup marinara sauce (60ml)

Instructions:

1. In a mixing bowl, combine ground turkey, feta, oregano, garlic, salt, and black pepper. Mix thoroughly until well combined. Shape the mixture into 4 evenly sized meatballs.
2. Heat olive oil in a skillet over medium heat. Add the meatballs and cook for 4-5 minutes per side, turning occasionally, until browned on all sides and fully cooked through.
3. Pour the marinara sauce into the skillet with the meatballs. Reduce the heat to low and simmer for 5 minutes, allowing the flavors to meld.

Nutritional Facts (Per Serving): Calories: 480 | Carbs: 10g | Protein: 24g | Fat: 22g | Fiber: 8g | Sodium: 500mg | Sugars: 4g

Chicken Shawarma with Garlic Tahini Sauce

Prep: 10 minutes | Cook: 20 minutes | Serves: 1

Ingredients:

- 4 oz chicken breast, sliced (115g)
- 1 tbsp olive oil (15ml)
- 1/2 tsp ground cumin (1g)
- 1/2 tsp smoked paprika (1g)
- 1/4 tsp turmeric (1g)
- 1 clove garlic, minced
- 1 tbsp tahini (15ml)
- 1 tsp lemon juice (5ml)
- 1/4 tsp sea salt (1g)
- 1/4 tsp black pepper (1g)

Instructions:

1. In a bowl, combine olive oil, cumin, paprika, turmeric, garlic, salt, and pepper.
2. Add the sliced chicken and toss to coat evenly. Let marinate for 10 minutes.
3. Heat a skillet over medium-high heat. Add the marinated chicken and cook for 4-5 minutes per side, or until golden brown and fully cooked. Remove from heat and set aside.
4. Whisk tahini, lemon juice, and 1 tbsp water until smooth, adding more water if needed.
5. Serve chicken with tahini sauce.

Nutritional Facts (Per Serving): Calories: 490 | Carbs: 8g | Protein: 25g | Fat: 21g | Fiber: 9g | Sodium: 450mg | Sugars: 2g

Spiced Ground Beef with Pine Nuts and Fresh Herbs

Prep: 10 minutes | Cook: 20 minutes | Serves: 1

Ingredients:

- 4 oz ground beef (115g)
- 1 tbsp pine nuts (10g)
- 1 clove garlic, minced
- 1/2 tsp ground cumin (1g)
- 1/2 tsp smoked paprika (1g)
- 1 tbsp olive oil (15ml)
- 1/4 tsp sea salt (1g)
- 1/4 tsp black pepper (1g)
- 1 tbsp chopped fresh parsley (2g)

Instructions:

1. Heat olive oil in a skillet over medium heat.
2. Add the ground beef to the skillet, breaking it apart with a spatula or wooden spoon and cook for 5-7 minutes.
3. Stir in the minced garlic, ground cumin, smoked paprika, sea salt, and black pepper. Cook for another 2-3 minutes until fragrant.
4. Add the pine nuts to the skillet and cook for 1-2 minutes, stirring frequently, until the nuts are lightly toasted and golden brown.
5. Remove from heat and sprinkle with fresh parsley before serving.

Nutritional Facts (Per Serving): Calories: 490 | Carbs: 8g | Protein: 24g | Fat: 22g | Fiber: 9g | Sodium: 500mg | Sugars: 2g

One-Pan Chicken with Mushrooms and White Wine Sauce

Prep: 10 minutes | Cook: 20 minutes | Serves: 1

Ingredients:

- 4 oz chicken breast, sliced (115g)
- 1 cup sliced mushrooms (100g)
- 1/4 cup dry white wine (60ml)
- 1 tbsp olive oil (15ml)
- 1 clove garlic, minced
- 1/4 cup chicken broth (60ml)
- 1/4 tsp sea salt (1g)
- 1/4 tsp black pepper (1g)
- 1 tsp chopped fresh thyme (2g)

Instructions:

1. Heat olive oil in a skillet over medium heat. Add chicken and cook for 4–5 minutes per side until golden. Remove and set aside.
2. Add garlic and mushrooms to the skillet, cooking for 3–4 minutes until softened. Deglaze the pan with white wine, scraping up browned bits. Simmer for 2–3 minutes, letting the wine reduce by half.
3. Stir in chicken broth, salt, pepper, and thyme. Return chicken to the pan and cook for 2–3 minutes until heated through.

Nutritional Facts (Per Serving): Calories: 480 | Carbs: 10g | Protein: 24g | Fat: 20g | Fiber: 8g | Sodium: 450mg | Sugars: 3g

Greek-Style Grilled Chicken with Lemon and Dill Yogurt

Prep: 10 minutes | Cook: 20 minutes | Serves: 1

Ingredients:

- 4 oz chicken breast (115g)
- 1 tbsp olive oil (15ml)
- Juice of 1/2 lemon (15ml)
- 1/4 cup plain Greek yogurt (60g)
- 1 tsp chopped fresh dill (2g)
- 1 clove garlic, minced
- 1/4 tsp sea salt (1g)
- 1/4 tsp black pepper (1g)

Instructions:

1. In a mixing bowl, combine olive oil, lemon juice, minced garlic, sea salt, and black pepper.
2. Add the chicken breast, ensuring it is well coated with the marinade. Cover and let it marinate for 10 minutes.
3. Heat a grill pan over medium heat and grill the chicken for 4-5 minutes per side until fully cooked.
4. In a small bowl, mix Greek yogurt, dill, and a pinch of salt to create the sauce.
5. Serve the grilled chicken drizzled with the dill yogurt sauce and garnish with extra dill if desired.

Nutritional Facts (Per Serving): Calories: 490 | Carbs: 5g | Protein: 25g | Fat: 21g | Fiber: 8g | Sodium: 450mg | Sugars: 2g

Quick Beef and Lentil Stir-Fry with Sumac

Prep: 10 minutes | Cook: 20 minutes | Serves: 1

Ingredients:

- 4 oz ground beef (115g)
- 1/4 cup cooked lentils (50g)
- 1 tbsp olive oil (15ml)
- 1 clove garlic, minced
- 1/4 tsp ground sumac (1g)
- 1/4 tsp smoked paprika (1g)
- 1/4 tsp sea salt (1g)
- 1/4 tsp black pepper (1g)
- 1 tbsp chopped parsley (2g)

Instructions:

1. Heat olive oil in a skillet over medium heat. Add ground beef and cook for 5-7 minutes, breaking it into crumbles.
2. Stir in the minced garlic and cook for 1 minute, allowing the garlic to become fragrant.
3. Add the cooked lentils, ground sumac, smoked paprika, sea salt, and black pepper. Stir well to combine and cook for another 3-4 minutes, stirring occasionally to ensure the flavors meld together.
4. Remove from heat and garnish with chopped parsley.

Nutritional Facts (Per Serving): Calories: 490 | Carbs: 10g | Protein: 24g | Fat: 22g | Fiber: 9g | Sodium: 450mg | Sugars: 2g

Chicken with Artichokes, Lemon, and Capers

Prep: 10 minutes | Cook: 20 minutes | Serves: 1

Ingredients:

- 4 oz chicken breast, sliced (115g)
- 1/2 cup canned artichoke hearts, drained and halved (75g)
- 1 tbsp olive oil (15ml)
- 1 tbsp capers (15g)
- Juice of 1/2 lemon (15ml)
- 1 clove garlic, minced
- 1/4 cup chicken broth (60ml)
- 1/4 tsp sea salt (1g)
- 1/4 tsp black pepper (1g)

Instructions:

1. Heat olive oil in a skillet over medium heat.
2. Add chicken slices and cook for 4-5 minutes per side until golden and cooked through. Remove and set aside.
3. In the same skillet, sauté garlic for 1 minute until fragrant. Add artichokes, capers, lemon juice, and chicken broth. Stir and cook for 3-4 minutes.
4. Return the chicken to the skillet and simmer for 2-3 minutes, letting the flavors meld.
5. Serve warm, garnished with extra lemon zest if desired.

Nutritional Facts (Per Serving): Calories: 490 | Carbs: 9g | Protein: 24g | Fat: 21g | Fiber: 9g | Sodium: 500mg | Sugars: 2g

Balsamic Glazed Turkey Cutlets with Rosemary

Prep: 10 minutes | Cook: 20 minutes | Serves: 1

Ingredients:

- 4 oz turkey cutlets (115g)
- 1 tbsp olive oil (15ml)
- 1 tbsp balsamic vinegar (15ml)
- 1 tsp chopped fresh rosemary (2g)
- 1 clove garlic, minced
- 1/4 tsp sea salt (1g)
- 1/4 tsp black pepper (1g)
- 1/4 cup chicken broth (60ml)

Instructions:

1. Heat olive oil in a skillet over medium heat.
2. Season turkey cutlets with salt and pepper and cook for 3-4 minutes per side until golden and cooked through. Remove and set aside.
3. In the same skillet, add garlic and sauté for 1 minute.
4. Stir in balsamic vinegar, rosemary, and chicken broth. Cook for 3-4 minutes until the sauce thickens slightly.
5. Return turkey to the skillet and coat with the glaze. Simmer for 2-3 minutes to absorb the flavors.

Nutritional Facts (Per Serving): Calories: 480 | Carbs: 7g | Protein: 25g | Fat: 20g | Fiber: 8g | Sodium: 450mg | Sugars: 3g

CHAPTER 11: SNACKS: Savory Mediterranean Appetizers and Dips

Roasted Eggplant and Tahini Spread with Garlic

Prep: 10 minutes | Cook: 20 minutes | Serves: 1

Ingredients:

- 1 small eggplant (200g)
- 1 tbsp tahini (15g)
- 1 clove garlic, minced
- 1 tsp olive oil (5ml)
- 1 tbsp lemon juice (15ml)
- Salt and pepper to taste

Instructions:

1. Preheat the oven to 400°F (200°C).
2. Slice the eggplant in half lengthwise and brush with olive oil. Roast cut side down on a baking sheet for 20 minutes or until tender.
3. Scoop out the roasted eggplant flesh and combine it with tahini, garlic, lemon juice, salt, and pepper in a food processor. Blend until smooth.
4. Season to taste; serve with veggies or crackers.

Nutritional Facts (Per Serving): Calories: 210 | Carbs: 18g | Protein: 8g | Fat: 10g | Fiber: 5g | Sodium: 280mg | Sugars: 3g

Cucumber and Mint Yogurt Dip

Prep: 10 minutes | Cook: 0 minutes | Serves: 1

Ingredients:

- 1/2 cup plain Greek yogurt (120g)
- 1/2 cucumber, grated (75g)
- 1 tbsp fresh mint, chopped (5g)
- 1 clove garlic, minced
- 1 tsp olive oil (5ml)
- 1 tsp lemon juice (5ml)
- Salt to taste

Instructions:

1. Squeeze the grated cucumber to remove excess water.
2. In a bowl, mix yogurt, cucumber, mint, garlic, olive oil, lemon juice, and a pinch of salt until well combined.
3. Serve chilled with warm pita bread, grilled whole-wheat flatbread, or crunchy whole-grain crackers.

Nutritional Facts (Per Serving): Calories: 190 | Carbs: 10g | Protein: 10g | Fat: 8g | Fiber: 4g | Sodium: 240mg | Sugars: 3g

Zaatar-Spiced Chickpea and Tahini Dip Enjoy

Prep: 10 minutes | Cook: 0 minutes | Serves: 1

Ingredients:

- 1/2 cup canned chickpeas, drained and rinsed (120g)
- 1 tbsp tahini (15g)
- 1 tbsp lemon juice (15ml)
- 1/2 clove garlic, minced
- 1/2 tsp zaatar spice blend (2g)
- 1 tsp olive oil (5ml)
- Salt and pepper to taste

Instructions:

1. Add the chickpeas, tahini, lemon juice, zaatar spice, minced garlic, and olive oil to a food processor or blender.
2. Blend the mixture on high speed until smooth and creamy. If the dip seems too thick, add water 1 tsp (5ml) at a time until the desired consistency is reached.
3. Add salt and pepper to taste. Blend again briefly to incorporate the seasoning.
4. Serve with warm naan, pita triangles, roasted sweet potato wedges, or toasted lavash chips.
5. Garnish with olive oil and zaatar, if desired.

Nutritional Facts (Per Serving): Calories: 210 | Carbs: 18g | Protein: 9g | Fat: 9g | Fiber: 5g | Sodium: 240mg | Sugars: 1g

Muhammara (Roasted Red Pepper and Walnut Dip)

Prep: 10 minutes | Cook: 10 minutes | Serves: 1

Ingredients:

- 1/2 cup roasted red peppers, drained (120g)
- 2 tbsp walnuts (15g)
- 1 tbsp olive oil (15ml)
- 1 tbsp lemon juice (15ml)
- 1/2 tsp ground cumin (2g)
- 1/2 clove garlic, minced
- Salt to taste

Instructions:

1. For enhanced flavor, lightly toast the walnuts in a dry skillet over medium heat for 2-3 minutes, stirring frequently to avoid burning. Allow them to cool.
2. In a food processor, combine the roasted red peppers, walnuts, olive oil, lemon juice, cumin, and minced garlic.
3. Blend the mixture on high speed until smooth and creamy. Scrape down the sides of the processor as needed for an even texture.
4. Add salt to taste, then blend briefly to incorporate. Adjust the consistency with a small amount of water, if necessary.

Nutritional Facts (Per Serving): Calories: 200 | Carbs: 12g | Protein: 8g | Fat: 9g | Fiber: 4g | Sodium: 250mg | Sugars: 2g

Labneh with Fresh Herbs, Olive Oil, and Pomegranate Seeds

Prep: 10 minutes | Cook: 0 minutes | Serves: 1

Ingredients:

- 1/2 cup labneh (120g)
- 1 tsp olive oil (5ml)
- 1 tbsp pomegranate seeds (15g)
- 1 tsp fresh parsley, chopped (2g)
- 1 tsp fresh mint, chopped (2g)
- Salt and pepper to taste

Instructions:

1. Spread the labneh evenly onto a small serving plate or shallow bowl using the back of a spoon to create a smooth and slightly indented surface.
2. Drizzle the olive oil over the surface of the labneh, letting it pool gently in the indentations.
3. Sprinkle the chopped parsley, mint, and pomegranate seeds evenly over the top.
4. Lightly season the labneh with salt and freshly ground pepper to taste.
5. Arrange the warm whole-wheat pita, toasted sesame crackers, or olive oil-brushed sourdough crostini around the labneh for dipping or spreading.

Nutritional Facts (Per Serving): Calories: 200 | Carbs: 9g | Protein: 9g | Fat: 10g | Fiber: 4g | Sodium: 250mg | Sugars: 3g

Roasted Red Pepper and Yogurt Dip with Sumac

Prep: 10 minutes | Cook: 5 minutes | Serves: 1

Ingredients:

- 1/2 cup plain Greek yogurt (120g)
- 1/4 cup roasted red peppers, chopped (60g)
- 1 tsp olive oil (5ml)
- 1/2 tsp sumac (2g)
- 1/2 clove garlic, minced
- Salt and pepper to taste

Instructions:

1. Add the yogurt, roasted red peppers, olive oil, garlic, and sumac to a blender or food processor.
2. Blend the ingredients on medium speed until the mixture becomes smooth and creamy. Stop occasionally to scrape down the sides of the blender for an even consistency.
3. Add salt and pepper to your liking, then blend briefly again to incorporate the seasoning.
4. Transfer the dip to a serving bowl. Sprinkle a pinch of sumac on top and drizzle with olive oil for extra flavor and presentation, if desired.
5. Pair the dip with crunchy vegetable crudités such as carrots, celery, radishes, and bell peppers.

Nutritional Facts (Per Serving): Calories: 190 | Carbs: 11g | Protein: 10g | Fat: 8g | Fiber: 4g | Sodium: 240mg | Sugars: 3g

CHAPTER 12: DESSERTS: Decadent Desserts with a Healthy Touch

Mediterranean Apple and Almond Clafoutis

Prep: 10 minutes | Cook: 20 minutes | Serves: 1

Ingredients:

- 1/4 cup whole grain flour (30g)
- 1/4 cup unsweetened almond milk (60ml)
- 1/2 apple, thinly sliced (75g)
- 1 large egg (50g)
- 1 tsp olive oil (5ml)
- 1/2 tsp vanilla extract (2.5ml)
- 1/2 tsp ground cinnamon (2g)
- 1/2 tsp honey (2g)
- Pinch of salt

Instructions:

1. Preheat oven to 375°F (190°C) and grease a small dish with olive oil.
2. Whisk whole grain flour, almond milk, egg, vanilla, cinnamon, honey, and salt until smooth.
3. Bake for 20 minutes or until the clafoutis is set and golden brown around the edges.

Nutritional Facts (Per Serving): Calories: 210 | Carbs: 16g | Protein: 9g | Fat: 10g | Fiber: 4g | Sodium: 240mg | Sugars: 3g

Orange and Almond Mediterranean Muffins

Prep: 10 minutes | Cook: 20 minutes | Serves: 1

Ingredients:

- 1/4 cup whole grain flour (30g)
- 1 large egg (50g)
- 1 tbsp orange juice (15ml)
- 1 tsp orange zest (2g)
- 1/2 tsp baking powder (2g)
- 1/2 tsp honey (2g)
- 1/2 tsp olive oil (5ml)
- Pinch of salt

Instructions:

1. Preheat the oven to 350°F (175°C). Line a muffin tin with one liner or lightly grease it.
2. Whisk whole grain flour, egg, orange juice, zest, baking powder, sweetener, oil, and salt.
3. Pour the batter into the prepared muffin tin. Bake for 18-20 minutes or until a toothpick inserted into the center comes out clean.

Nutritional Facts (Per Serving): Calories: 200 | Carbs: 8g | Protein: 9g | Fat: 10g | Fiber: 4g | Sodium: 230mg | Sugars: 2g

Mediterranean Olive Oil and Citrus Cake

Prep: 10 minutes | Cook: 20 minutes | Serves: 1

Ingredients:

- 3 tbsp all-purpose flour (24g)
- 1 1/2 tbsp olive oil (20ml)
- 1 tbsp honey (10g)
- 1 tbsp orange juice (15ml)
- 1/2 tsp orange zest (1g)
- 1/4 tsp baking powder (1g)
- 1 large egg white (30g)
- Pinch of salt

Instructions:

1. Preheat the oven to 350°F (180°C) and grease a small ramekin or baking dish.
2. In a bowl, whisk the olive oil, orange juice, orange zest, and egg white.
3. In a separate bowl, mix the flour, baking powder, salt, and sweetener. Gradually combine the wet and dry ingredients.
4. Pour the batter into the ramekin and bake for 18-20 minutes or until a toothpick comes out clean.
5. Cool slightly before serving.

Nutritional Facts (Per Serving): Calories: 200 | Carbs: 19g | Protein: 9g | Fat: 8g | Fiber: 5g | Sodium: 220mg | Sugars: 3g

Chocolate and Olive Oil Cake with Orange Glaze

Prep: 10 minutes | Cook: 20 minutes | Serves: 1

Ingredients:

- 3 tbsp whole grain flourr (24g)
- 1 1/2 tbsp olive oil (20ml)
- 1 tbsp cocoa powder (8g)
- 1 tbsp honey (10g)
- 1 large egg white (30g)
- 1/4 tsp baking powder (1g)
- Pinch of salt

For the Glaze:
- 1 tsp orange juice (5ml)
- 1/2 tsp honey (2g)

Instructions:

1. Preheat oven to 350°F (180°C); grease ramekin.
2. Whisk olive oil, egg white, sweetener, and cocoa powder.
3. Combine whole grain flour, baking powder, and salt; fold into wet mixture.
4. Pour the batter into the ramekin and bake for 18-20 minutes or until set.
5. For the glaze, mix orange juice and honey until smooth. Drizzle over the cooled cake.

Nutritional Facts (Per Serving): Calories: 210 | Carbs: 11g | Protein: 8g | Fat: 9g | Fiber: 4g | Sodium: 200mg | Sugars: 2g

Raisin and Walnut Greek Easter Cookies (Koulourakia)

Prep: 10 minutes | Cook: 15 minutes | Serves: 1

Ingredients:

- 1 tbsp unsalted butter (14g)
- 2 tbsp honey (30g)
- 1 large egg (50g)
- 1/4 tsp vanilla extract (1.25ml)
- 1/4 cupwhole grain flour (28g)
- 1 tbsp chopped walnuts (10g)
- 1 tbsp raisins (10g)
- 1/4 tsp baking powder (1g)

Instructions:

1. Preheat oven to 350°F (175°C). Line a baking sheet with parchment paper.
2. Cream butter and honey in a bowl until light and fluffy.
3. Mix in the egg and vanilla extract until well combined. Fold in whole grain flour, baking powder, walnuts, and raisins.
4. Use about 1 tablespoon of dough for each cookie, shaping it into small twists or rounds. Place them on the prepared baking sheet.
5. Bake for 12–15 minutes or until golden.

Nutritional Facts (Per Serving): Calories: 210 | Carbs: 12g | Protein: 8g | Fat: 10g | Fiber: 4g | Sodium: 200mg | Sugars: 3g

Saffron and Pistachio Muffins with Yogurt

Prep: 10 minutes | Cook: 20 minutes | Serves: 1

Ingredients:

- 1 tbsp unsalted butter (14g)
- 2 tbsp honey(30g)
- 1/4 cup whole grain flour (28g)
- 1 tbsp plain Greek yogurt (15g)
- 1 large egg (50g)
- 1/4 tsp saffron threads (0.5g), soaked in 1 tbsp warm water (15ml)
- 1 tbsp chopped pistachios (10g)
- 1/4 tsp baking powder (1g)

Instructions:

1. Preheat oven to 350°F (175°C). Grease a muffin tin or line with a muffin liner.
2. In a bowl, whisk together butter and honey until smooth. Mix in egg, yogurt, and saffron water until fully combined.
3. Fold in whole grain flour, baking powder, and pistachios.
4. Pour the batter into the prepared muffin tin and bake for 18-20 minutes or until a toothpick inserted into the center comes out clean.

Nutritional Facts (Per Serving): Calories: 200 | Carbs: 10g | Protein: 9g | Fat: 9g | Fiber: 4g | Sodium: 220mg | Sugars: 2g

Tahini and Maple Syrup Brownies

Prep: 10 minutes | Cook: 15 minutes | Serves: 1

Ingredients:

- 2 tbsp tahini (30g)
- 1 tbsp honey (15g)
- 1 tbsp maple syrup (15ml)
- 1 large egg (50g)
- 2 tbsp whole grain flour (14g)
- 1 tsp cocoa powder (5g)
- 1/4 tsp baking powder (1g)
- Pinch of sea salt

Instructions:

1. Preheat oven to 350°F (175°C). Grease a small baking dish or line with parchment paper.
2. In a bowl, whisk together tahini, egg, honey, maple syrup, and until smooth.
3. Gently fold in the whole grain flour, cocoa powder, baking powder, and a pinch of sea salt. Stir until the batter is smooth and well-mixed.
4. Pour the batter into the prepared baking dish, spreading it evenly with a spatula.
5. Bake for 12-15 minutes, or until the center is just set and a toothpick inserted into the middle comes out with a few moist crumbs.

Nutritional Facts (Per Serving): Calories: 200 | Carbs: 12g | Protein: 9g | Fat: 9g | Fiber: 5g | Sodium: 220mg | Sugars: 3g

Hazelnut and Cocoa Nib Cookies with Olive Oil

Prep: 10 minutes | Cook: 15 minutes | Serves: 1

Ingredients:

- 1 tbsp olive oil (15ml)
- 2 tbsp honey (30g)
- 1 large egg (50g)
- 2 tbsp hazelnut flour (14g)
- 1 tbsp cocoa nibs (10g)
- 1/4 tsp baking powder (1g)
- Pinch of sea salt

Instructions:

1. Preheat oven to 350°F (175°C). Line a baking sheet with parchment paper.
2. In a bowl, whisk together olive oil, honey, and egg until smooth.
3. Stir in hazelnut flour, cocoa nibs, baking powder, and sea salt.
4. Drop spoonfuls of dough onto the baking sheet and flatten slightly.
5. Bake for 12-15 minutes or until golden. Cool before serving.

Nutritional Facts (Per Serving): Calories: 210 | Carbs: 10g | Protein: 8g | Fat: 10g | Fiber: 4g | Sodium: 200mg | Sugars: 2g

Whole Wheat Banana and Honey Cake

Prep: 10 minutes | Cook: 15 minutes | Serves: 1

Ingredients:

- 2 tbsp mashed ripe banana (30g)
- 1 tbsp honey (15ml)
- 2 tbsp whole wheat flour (14g)
- 1 large egg (50g)
- 1/4 tsp baking powder (1g)
- 1/4 tsp ground cinnamon (0.5g)
- Pinch of sea salt

Instructions:

1. Set it to 350°F (175°C). Grease a small ramekin or baking dish.
2. In a bowl, mix mashed banana, honey, and egg until smooth.
3. Add whole wheat flour, baking powder, cinnamon, and a pinch of sea salt. Stir until just combined.
4. Pour the batter into the prepared dish and bake for 12-15 minutes, or until a toothpick inserted in the center comes out clean.
5. Let the cake cool slightly before serving warm.

Nutritional Facts (Per Serving): Calories: 200 | Carbs: 26g | Protein: 8g | Fat: 7g | Fiber: 5g | Sodium: 200mg | Sugars: 4g

Almond and Apricot Bars

Prep: 10 minutes | Cook: 15 minutes | Serves: 1

Ingredients:

- 2 tbsp whole grain flour(14g)
- 1 tbsp chopped dried apricots (10g)
- 1 tbsp lhoney (15g)
- 1 tbsp unsweetened almond butter (16g)
- 1 large egg white (30g)
- 1/4 tsp vanilla extract (1.25ml)
- Pinch of sea salt

Instructions:

1. Heat to 350°F (175°C). Line a small baking sheet with parchment paper.
2. In a bowl, combine whole grain flour, chopped apricots, and a pinch of sea salt.
3. In a separate bowl, whisk together almond butter, honey, egg white, and vanilla extract.
4. Mix wet ingredients into the dry ingredients until a sticky dough forms.
5. Press the dough into a small rectangle on the baking sheet.
6. Bake for 12-15 minutes, or until edges are golden brown. Cool before slicing into bars.

Nutritional Facts (Per Serving): Calories: 210 | Carbs: 14g | Protein: 9g | Fat: 9g | Fiber: 4g | Sodium: 220mg | Sugars: 3g

CHAPTER 13: DESSERTS: Effortless No-Bake Mediterranean Sweets

No-Bake Greek Yogurt Cheesecake with Honey and Walnuts

Prep: 10 minutes | Cook: 0 minutes | Serves: 1

Ingredients:

- 2 tbsp whole grain flour (14g)
- 1/2 tsp honey (2.5ml)
- 2 tbsp plain Greek yogurt (30g)
- 1 tbsp cream cheese (15g)
- 1/4 tsp vanilla extract (1.25ml)
- 1 tsp chopped walnuts (5g)
- Pinch of sea salt

Instructions:

1. Mix whole grain flour, honey, a pinch of salt. Press into a small ramekin or glass.
2. Whisk together Greek yogurt, cream cheese, vanilla extract, and the remaining honey until smooth. Spread the mixture over the crust.
3. Top with walnuts and chill for 10 minutes.

Nutritional Facts (Per Serving): Calories: 200 | Carbs: 12g | Protein: 9g | Fat: 9g | Fiber: 4g | Sodium: 220mg | Sugars: 3g

Tahini and Dark Chocolate Truffles with Sesame Crunch

Prep: 10 minutes | Cook: 5 minutes | Serves: 1

Ingredients:

- 1 tbsp tahini (15g)
- 1 tbsp honeyr (15g)
- 1/2 tsp sesame seeds (2g)
- 1 tbsp dark chocolate chips, melted (15g)
- Pinch of sea salt

Instructions:

1. In a small bowl, mix tahini and honey until smooth. Stir in melted dark chocolate until fully combined. Roll into small balls.
2. Sprinkle sesame seeds and a pinch of sea salt over the truffles. Press lightly to adhere.
3. Refrigerate the truffles for 10 minutes to firm up before serving.

Nutritional Facts (Per Serving): Calories: 200 | Carbs: 8g | Protein: 8g | Fat: 10g | Fiber: 5g | Sodium: 200mg | Sugars: 3g

Saffron and Almond Milk Panna Cotta with Cardamom

Prep: 10 minutes | Cook: 5 minutes | Serves: 1

Ingredients:

- 1/2 cup unsweetened almond milk (120ml)
- 1/4 tsp saffron threads (0.5g)
- 1/4 tsp ground cardamom (0.5g)
- 1 tbsp honeyr (15g)
- 1/2 tsp unflavored gelatin (2g)

Instructions:

1. In a small saucepan, combine almond milk, saffron, and cardamom. Warm over low heat, stirring occasionally, until the saffron infuses and the milk becomes fragrant. Do not let it boil.
2. Remove the saucepan from the heat and stir in the honey until fully dissolved.
3. Sprinkle the gelatin over 1 tbsp of cold water in a small bowl. Let it sit for 1-2 minutes until it softens.
4. Stir the bloomed gelatin into the warm almond milk mixture until completely dissolved.
5. Pour the mixture into a small ramekin or glass. Refrigerate for at least 2 hours, or until the panna cotta is firm.

Nutritional Facts (Per Serving): Calories: 200 | Carbs: 8g | Protein: 8g | Fat: 8g | Fiber: 4g | Sodium: 220mg | Sugars: 2g

No-Bake Chocolate and Olive Oil Tart with Sea Salt

Prep: 10 minutes | Cook: 5 minutes | Serves: 1

Ingredients:

- 2 tbsp whole grain flour (14g)
- 1/2 tsp honey (2.5g)
- 1 tsp olive oil (5ml)
- 1 tbsp dark chocolate chips, melted (15g)
- Pinch of sea salt

Instructions:

1. In a small bowl, mix whole grain flour, honey, and olive oil until it resembles wet sand. Press the mixture firmly into the base of a small tart pan, ramekin, or glass to form the crust.
2. Place the dark chocolate chips in a microwave-safe bowl and melt in 15-second intervals, stirring after each, until smooth.
3. Pour melted chocolate over the crust and spread evenly.
4. Sprinkle a pinch of sea salt over the chocolate layer for added flavor.
5. Refrigerate for 15-20 minutes, or until the chocolate is firm.

Nutritional Facts (Per Serving): Calories: 210 | Carbs: 10g | Protein: 9g | Fat: 10g | Fiber: 4g | Sodium: 250mg | Sugars: 3g

Pomegranate and Pistachio Ricotta Mousse

Prep: 10 minutes | Cook: 0 minutes | Serves: 1

Ingredients:

- 1/4 cup ricotta cheese (60g)
- 1 tbsp honey (15g)
- 1/4 tsp vanilla extract (1.25ml)
- 1 tbsp fresh pomegranate seeds (10g)
- 1 tsp crushed pistachios (5g)

Instructions:

1. In a medium bowl, combine ricotta, honey, and vanilla extract. Use a whisk or hand mixer to whip the mixture until it becomes light and fluffy. This should take about 2-3 minutes.
2. Spoon the whipped ricotta mixture into a small serving glass or dish, smoothing the top with the back of a spoon.
3. Sprinkle the pomegranate seeds evenly over the ricotta mousse. Follow with the crushed pistachios for a crunchy contrast.
4. Place the mousse in the refrigerator for 5-10 minutes to let the flavors meld.

Nutritional Facts (Per Serving): Calories: 200 | Carbs: 10g | Protein: 9g | Fat: 9g | Fiber: 4g | Sodium: 220mg | Sugars: 3g

Rosewater and Fig Chia Pudding with Toasted Almonds

Prep: 5 minutes | Cook: 0 minutes | Serves: 1

Ingredients:

- 2 tbsp chia seeds (30g)
- 1/2 cup unsweetened almond milk (120ml)
- 1/4 tsp rosewater (1.25ml)
- 1 small fig, diced (20g)
- 1 tsp honey (5g)
- 1 tsp toasted sliced almonds (5g)

Instructions:

1. In a jar, mix chia seeds, almond milk, rosewater, and sweetener. Stir well to combine.
2. Let the mixture sit for 5 minutes, then stir again to prevent the chia seeds from clumping.
3. Cover the jar or bowl with a lid or plastic wrap and refrigerate for at least 2 hours, or overnight if preparing in advance. The chia seeds will absorb the liquid and create a pudding-like consistency.
4. Toast almonds in a dry skillet over medium heat for 2 minutes. Cool.
5. Once the pudding has set, give it a quick stir. Top with diced fig and toasted almonds before serving.

Nutritional Facts (Per Serving): Calories: 210 | Carbs: 14g | Protein: 8g | Fat: 9g | Fiber: 5g | Sodium: 200mg | Sugars: 3g

CHAPTER 14: DINNER: Refreshing Mediterranean Salad Creations

Roasted Eggplant and Lentil Salad with Basil and Balsamic

Prep: 10 minutes | Cook: 20 minutes | Serves: 1

Ingredients:

- 1 small eggplant, diced (200g)
- 1/2 cup cooked lentils (120g)
- 1 tbsp olive oil (15ml)
- 1 tbsp balsamic vinegar (15ml)
- 1/4 tsp sea salt (1.5g)
- 1/4 cup fresh basil leaves, chopped (10g)
- 1 tbsp pine nuts, toasted (15g)
- 1/4 tsp black pepper (0.5g)

Instructions:

1. Preheat oven to 425°F (220°C). Toss eggplant with oil, salt, and pepper; roast 20 mins, turning once.
2. In a bowl, combine roasted eggplant, cooked lentils, balsamic vinegar, and basil. Mix gently.
3. Top with toasted pine nuts and serve.

Nutritional Facts (Per Serving): Calories: 360 | Carbs: 28g | Protein: 20g | Fat: 15g | Fiber: 8g | Sodium: 450mg | Sugars: 5g

Tomato and Mozzarella Caprese with Basil and Olive Oil

Prep: 5 minutes | Cook: 0 minutes | Serves: 1

Ingredients:

- 1 medium tomato, sliced (150g)
- 3 oz fresh mozzarella, sliced (85g)
- 1 tbsp olive oil (15ml)
- 1 tbsp balsamic vinegar (15ml)
- 1/4 cup fresh basil leaves (10g)
- 1/4 tsp sea salt (1.5g)
- 1/4 tsp black pepper (0.5g)

Instructions:

1. Slice the tomato and mozzarella evenly, then alternate the slices on a plate to create a visually appealing pattern.
2. Drizzle the olive oil and balsamic vinegar evenly over the tomato and mozzarella slices.
3. Sprinkle with salt, pepper, and garnish with fresh basil.

Nutritional Facts (Per Serving): Calories: 370 | Carbs: 9g | Protein: 21g | Fat: 25g | Fiber: 7g | Sodium: 500mg | Sugars: 5g

Cucumber and Mint Yogurt Salad with Sumac

Prep: 10 minutes | Cook: 0 minutes | Serves: 1

Ingredients:

- 1 small cucumber, diced (120g)
- 1/2 cup plain Greek yogurt (120g)
- 1/4 tsp ground sumac (1g)
- 1 tbsp fresh mint leaves, chopped (5g)
- 1/4 tsp sea salt (1.5g)
- 1/4 tsp black pepper (0.5g)
- 1 tsp olive oil (5ml)

Instructions:

1. Peel the cucumber and dice it into small, even cubes. Place the cucumber in a medium bowl.
2. Add the Greek yogurt and chopped mint leaves to the bowl with the cucumber.
3. Sprinkle ground sumac, sea salt, and black pepper evenly over the mixture.
4. Stir gently until all the ingredients are thoroughly combined and the yogurt coats the cucumber evenly.
5. Drizzle olive oil on top as a finishing touch. Serve immediately as a refreshing side or light snack.

Nutritional Facts (Per Serving): Calories: 310 | Carbs: 10g | Protein: 19g | Fat: 15g | Fiber: 7g | Sodium: 420mg | Sugars: 4g

Bulgur and Roasted Zucchini Salad with Lemon Dressing

Prep: 10 minutes | Cook: 15 minutes | Serves: 1

Ingredients:

- 1/4 cup dry bulgur wheat (50g)
- 1/2 medium zucchini, diced (100g)
- 1 tbsp olive oil, divided (15ml)
- Juice of 1/2 lemon (15ml)
- 1/4 tsp sea salt (1.5g)
- 1/4 tsp black pepper (0.5g)
- 1 tbsp parsley, chopped (5g)

Instructions:

1. Cook bulgur according to package instructions, fluff with a fork, and cool slightly.
2. Preheat oven to 400°F (200°C). Toss zucchini with 1/2 tbsp olive oil, salt, and pepper, then roast on a parchment-lined sheet for 10-15 minutes, stirring once.
3. In a bowl, mix bulgur, roasted zucchini, parsley, remaining olive oil, and lemon juice. Season with salt and pepper. Toss and serve warm or at room temperature.

Nutritional Facts (Per Serving): Calories: 360 | Carbs: 28g | Protein: 20g | Fat: 14g | Fiber: 8g | Sodium: 450mg | Sugars: 4g

Warm Roasted Beet and Goat Cheese Salad with Citrus Dressing

Prep: 10 minutes | Cook: 20 minutes | Serves: 1

Ingredients:

- 1 medium beet, roasted and sliced (150g)
- 1 oz goat cheese, crumbled (30g)
- 2 cups mixed greens (60g)
- 1 tbsp olive oil (15ml)
- 1 tbsp orange juice (15ml)
- 1/2 tsp orange zest (1g)
- 1/4 tsp sea salt (1.5g)
- 1/4 tsp black pepper (0.5g)

Instructions:

1. Preheat the oven to 400°F (200°C), wrap the beet in foil, and roast for 20 minutes or until tender, then let it cool slightly before peeling and slicing thinly.
2. In a small bowl, whisk together olive oil, orange juice, orange zest, salt, and pepper until the dressing is smooth and well-combined.
3. Arrange mixed greens on a serving plate, layer the roasted beet slices on top, and sprinkle with crumbled goat cheese.
4. Drizzle the citrus dressing evenly over the salad, ensuring all components are lightly coated.

Nutritional Facts (Per Serving): Calories: 330 | Carbs: 22g | Protein: 18g | Fat: 16g | Fiber: 8g | Sodium: 450mg | Sugars: 5g

Bulgur and Grilled Chicken Salad with Pomegranate Vinaigrette

Prep: 10 minutes | Cook: 20 minutes | Serves: 1

Ingredients:

- 1/4 cup dry bulgur wheat (50g)
- 4 oz grilled chicken breast, sliced (120g)
- 1/4 cup pomegranate seeds (40g)
- 2 cups mixed greens (60g)
- 1 tbsp olive oil (15ml)
- 1 tbsp pomegranate juice (15ml)
- 1/4 tsp sea salt (1.5g)
- 1/4 tsp black pepper (0.5g)

Instructions:

1. Cook the bulgur by soaking it in boiling water for 10-12 minutes, then drain, fluff with a fork, and allow it to cool slightly.
2. Season the chicken breast with salt and pepper, grill over medium heat for 4-5 minutes per side until fully cooked, and slice into thin strips.
3. Whisk olive oil, pomegranate juice, salt, and pepper until smooth.
4. Arrange greens, top with bulgur, chicken, pomegranate seeds, and drizzle vinaigrette.

Nutritional Facts (Per Serving): Calories: 370 | Carbs: 25g | Protein: 23g | Fat: 15g | Fiber: 8g | Sodium: 500mg | Sugars: 5g

Arugula and Beef Salad with Sun-Dried Tomatoes and Parmesan

Prep: 10 minutes | Cook: 15 minutes | Serves: 1

Ingredients:

- 4 oz lean beef steak, grilled and sliced (120g)
- 2 cups arugula (60g)
- 2 sun-dried tomatoes, chopped (15g)
- 1 tbsp grated Parmesan cheese (10g)
- 1 tbsp olive oil (15ml)
- 1 tsp balsamic vinegar (5ml)
- 1/4 tsp sea salt (1.5g)
- 1/4 tsp black pepper (0.5g)

Instructions:

1. Season the beef with salt and pepper, grill over medium heat for 4-5 minutes per side until cooked to your desired doneness, then let it rest for 5 minutes before slicing thinly against the grain.
2. Arrange arugula on a plate, top with beef, sun-dried tomatoes, and Parmesan.
3. In a small bowl, whisk together olive oil and balsamic vinegar until well combined, then drizzle the dressing evenly over the salad.

Nutritional Facts (Per Serving): Calories: 350 | Carbs: 8g | Protein: 24g | Fat: 16g | Fiber: 7g | Sodium: 500mg | Sugars: 4g

Lentil and Roasted Chicken Salad with Garlic Yogurt Dressing

Prep: 10 minutes | Cook: 20 minutes | Serves: 1

Ingredients:

- 1/2 cup cooked lentils (120g)
- 4 oz roasted chicken breast, sliced (120g)
- 2 cups mixed greens (60g)
- 1 tbsp plain Greek yogurt (15g)
- 1 tsp olive oil (5ml)
- 1 clove garlic, minced (3g)
- Juice of 1/2 lemon (15ml)
- 1/4 tsp sea salt (1.5g)
- 1/4 tsp black pepper (0.5g)

Instructions:

1. Arrange the cooked lentils, sliced roasted chicken breast, and mixed greens evenly on a serving plate to create a layered base.
2. In a small bowl, whisk together the Greek yogurt, olive oil, minced garlic, lemon juice, salt, and pepper until the mixture becomes creamy and smooth.
3. Drizzle the garlic yogurt dressing evenly over the salad, ensuring all components are lightly coated, and toss gently to combine.

Nutritional Facts (Per Serving): Calories: 370 | Carbs: 22g | Protein: 25g | Fat: 15g | Fiber: 8g | Sodium: 450mg | Sugars: 3g

Warm Farro and Grilled Lamb Salad with Lemon and Herbs

Prep: 10 minutes | Cook: 20 minutes | Serves: 1

Ingredients:

- 1/4 cup cooked farro (50g)
- 4 oz grilled lamb loin, sliced (120g)
- 2 cups mixed greens (60g)
- 1 tbsp olive oil (15ml)
- Juice of 1/2 lemon (15ml)
- 1 tsp lemon zest (2g)
- 1 tbsp fresh parsley, chopped (5g)
- 1/4 tsp sea salt (1.5g)
- 1/4 tsp black pepper (0.5g)

Instructions:

1. Cook farro according to package instructions, then drain and keep warm.
2. Season the lamb loin with salt and pepper, grill over medium heat for 4-5 minutes per side until medium-rare, let rest, and slice thinly.
3. In a small bowl, whisk together olive oil, lemon juice, and zest to make the dressing.
4. On a plate, layer mixed greens, warm farro, and lamb slices, then drizzle with the lemon dressing and sprinkle with parsley.

Nutritional Facts (Per Serving): Calories: 360 | Carbs: 22g | Protein: 24g | Fat: 15g | Fiber: 8g | Sodium: 450mg | Sugars: 3g

Chicken and Artichoke Salad with Basil and Pine Nuts

Prep: 10 minutes | Cook: 15 minutes | Serves: 1

Ingredients:

- 4 oz cooked chicken breast, shredded (120g)
- 1/2 cup canned artichoke hearts, chopped (85g)
- 2 cups arugula (60g)
- 1 tbsp olive oil (15ml)
- Juice of 1/2 lemon (15ml)
- 1 tbsp pine nuts, toasted (15g)
- 1 tbsp fresh basil, chopped (5g)
- 1/4 tsp sea salt (1.5g)
- 1/4 tsp black pepper (0.5g)

Instructions:

1. Combine shredded chicken, chopped artichoke hearts, and arugula on a plate.
2. Toast pine nuts in a dry skillet over medium heat for 1-2 minutes, stirring constantly, until golden.
3. In a small bowl, whisk together olive oil, lemon juice, salt, and pepper to create the dressing.
4. Drizzle the dressing over the salad, then sprinkle with toasted pine nuts and fresh basil.

Nutritional Facts (Per Serving): Calories: 370 | Carbs: 12g | Protein: 25g | Fat: 16g | Fiber: 7g | Sodium: 480mg | Sugars: 3g

CHAPTER 15: DINNER: Easy One-Pan Dinners for Busy Evenings

Mediterranean One-Pan Balsamic Chicken with Roasted Tomatoes

Prep: 10 minutes | Cook: 20 minutes | Serves: 1

Ingredients:

- 4 oz boneless, skinless chicken breast (120g)
- 1/2 cup cherry tomatoes, halved (100g)
- 1 tbsp balsamic vinegar (15ml)
- 1 tbsp olive oil (15ml)
- 1 clove garlic, minced (3g)
- 1/4 tsp dried oregano (0.5g)
- 1/4 tsp sea salt (1.5g)
- 1/4 tsp black pepper (0.5g)

Instructions:

1. Heat olive oil in a skillet over medium heat, season chicken with salt, pepper, and oregano, and sear for 4-5 minutes per side.
2. Add tomatoes, garlic, and balsamic vinegar, then cook for 8-10 minutes until chicken is done and tomatoes soften.

Nutritional Facts (Per Serving): Calories: 360 | Carbs: 9g | Protein: 24g | Fat: 15g | Fiber: 8g | Sodium: 450mg | Sugars: 5g

One-Skillet Moroccan Lamb with Olives and Peppers

Prep: 10 minutes | Cook: 20 minutes | Serves: 1

Ingredients:

- 4 oz ground lamb (120g)
- 1/2 red bell pepper, sliced (75g)
- 1/4 cup pitted green olives, sliced (30g)
- 1 tbsp olive oil (15ml)
- 1 clove garlic, minced (3g)
- 1/4 tsp ground cumin (0.5g)
- 1/4 tsp ground paprika (0.5g)
- 1/4 tsp sea salt (1.5g)
- 1/4 tsp black pepper (0.5g)

Instructions:

1. Heat olive oil in a skillet, add lamb, season with spices, and cook for 6-8 minutes, breaking into pieces.
2. Add sliced bell peppers, minced garlic, and olives to the skillet, and cook for an additional 6-8 minutes until the peppers are tender.

Nutritional Facts (Per Serving): Calories: 370 | Carbs: 8g | Protein: 23g | Fat: 17g | Fiber: 7g | Sodium: 500mg | Sugars: 4g

Rosemary and Olive Oil Turkey with Roasted Cauliflower

Prep: 10 minutes | Cook: 20 minutes | Serves: 1

Ingredients:

- 4 oz turkey breast, sliced (120g)
- 1 cup cauliflower florets (100g)
- 1/2 tsp dried rosemary (1g)
- 1 tbsp olive oil, divided (15ml)
- 1/4 tsp garlic powder (0.5g)
- 1/4 tsp sea salt (1.5g)
- 1/4 tsp black pepper (0.5g)

Instructions:

1. Preheat oven to 400°F (200°C). Line a baking sheet with parchment paper for easy cleanup.
2. Toss cauliflower florets with 1/2 tbsp olive oil, salt, and garlic powder until evenly coated, then spread in a single layer on the baking sheet and roast for 15-20 minutes, flipping halfway, until tender and golden.
3. Heat the remaining olive oil in a skillet over medium heat. Season turkey with rosemary, salt, and pepper on both sides, then sear in the skillet for 4-5 minutes per side until golden and fully cooked.

Nutritional Facts (Per Serving): Calories: 380 | Carbs: 28g | Protein: 22g | Fat: 17g | Fiber: 7g | Sodium: 450mg | Sugars: 2g

One-Pan Mediterranean Chicken with Artichokes and Capers

Prep: 10 minutes | Cook: 20 minutes | Serves: 1

Ingredients:

- 4 oz boneless, skinless chicken breast (120g)
- 1/2 cup canned artichoke hearts, drained and halved (85g)
- 1 tbsp capers (15g)
- 1 tbsp olive oil (15ml)
- Juice of 1/2 lemon (15ml)
- 1 clove garlic, minced (3g)
- 1/4 tsp sea salt (1.5g)
- 1/4 tsp black pepper (0.5g)

Instructions:

1. Heat olive oil in a skillet over medium heat. Season chicken with salt and pepper on both sides, then sear for 4-5 minutes per side until golden brown.
2. Add artichokes, capers, and minced garlic to the skillet, stirring to combine with the chicken and allow the flavors to meld.
3. Pour lemon juice over the mixture and cook for 8-10 minutes, stirring occasionally, until the chicken is fully cooked, artichokes are tender, and the sauce thickens slightly.

Nutritional Facts (Per Serving): Calories: 370 | Carbs: 8g | Protein: 23g | Fat: 16g | Fiber: 7g | Sodium: 480mg | Sugars: 3g

Garlic and Cumin-Spiced Beef with Roasted Sweet Potatoes

Prep: 10 minutes | Cook: 20 minutes | Serves: 1

Ingredients:

- 4 oz (120g) lean ground beef
- 1/2 cup (120g) cooked chickpeas
- 1 tbsp (15ml) olive oil, divided
- 1 clove garlic, minced (3g)
- 1/2 tsp ground cumin (1g)
- 1/4 tsp sea salt (1.5g)
- 1/4 tsp black pepper (0.5g)
- 1/2 tsp smoked paprika (1g)

Instructions:

1. Heat 1/2 tbsp olive oil in a skillet over medium heat.
2. Add ground beef, season with salt, pepper, and cumin, and cook for 6-8 minutes, breaking it into pieces.
3. In a separate bowl, toss chickpeas with 1/2 tbsp olive oil, garlic, and paprika.
4. Spread chickpeas on a baking sheet and roast at 400°F (200°C) for 10 minutes, stirring once.
5. Serve the beef over roasted chickpeas, garnished with fresh parsley if desired.

Nutritional Facts (Per Serving): Calories: 370 | Carbs: 18g | Protein: 23g | Fat: 16g | Fiber: 8g | Sodium: 480mg | Sugars: 3g

Tomato and Basil One-Pan Turkey with Lentils

Prep: 10 minutes | Cook: 20 minutes | Serves: 1

Ingredients:

- 4 oz ground turkey (120g)
- 1/2 cup cooked lentils (120g)
- 1/2 cup diced tomatoes (100g)
- 1 tbsp olive oil (15ml)
- 1 clove garlic, minced (3g)
- 1 tbsp fresh basil, chopped (5g)
- 1/4 tsp sea salt (1.5g)
- 1/4 tsp black pepper (0.5g)

Instructions:

1. Heat olive oil in a skillet over medium heat, add ground turkey, and cook for 6-8 minutes, breaking it into small pieces, until it is evenly browned and cooked through.
2. Add minced garlic to the skillet and stir for 1 minute until fragrant.
3. Stir in diced tomatoes and lentils, season with salt and pepper, and simmer for 8-10 minutes, stirring occasionally to meld the flavors.
4. Remove from heat, sprinkle with basil, and let rest for 2 minutes before serving.

Nutritional Facts (Per Serving): Calories: 360 | Carbs: 20g | Protein: 24g | Fat: 15g | Fiber: 8g | Sodium: 450mg | Sugars: 4g

CHAPTER 16: DINNER: Coastal Favorites: Fish and Seafood Specialties

Shrimp Saganaki (Greek Shrimp in Tomato and Feta Sauce)

Prep: 10 minutes | Cook: 20 minutes | Serves: 1

Ingredients:

- 4 oz large shrimp, peeled and deveined (120g)
- 1/2 cup diced tomatoes (100g)
- 1 oz crumbled feta cheese (30g)
- 1 tbsp olive oil (15ml)
- 1 clove garlic, minced (3g)
- 1/4 tsp dried oregano (0.5g)
- 1/4 tsp sea salt (1.5g)
- 1/4 tsp black pepper (0.5g)

Instructions:

1. Heat olive oil in a skillet, sauté garlic for 1 minute. Add tomatoes, oregano, salt, and pepper; simmer for 5-6 minutes.
2. Add shrimp and cook 3-4 minutes per side until pink. Sprinkle with feta, cover, and cook 2-3 minutes until softened.

Nutritional Facts (Per Serving): Calories: 380 | Carbs: 2g | Protein: 23g | Fat: 17g | Fiber: 1g | Sodium: 480mg | Sugars: 0g

Roasted Mackerel with Olive and Sun-Dried Tomato Relish

Prep: 10 minutes | Cook: 20 minutes | Serves: 1

Ingredients:

- 1 small mackerel, cleaned and filleted (150g)
- 1 tbsp olive oil, divided (15ml)
- 2 sun-dried tomatoes, chopped (15g)
- 1 tbsp pitted black olives, chopped (15g)
- Juice of 1/2 lemon (15ml)
- 1 clove garlic, minced (3g)
- 1/4 tsp sea salt (1.5g)
- 1/4 tsp black pepper (0.5g)

Instructions:

1. Preheat oven to 400°F (200°C).
2. Drizzle mackerel with 1/2 tbsp olive oil, season, and roast for 15-20 minutes.
3. Mix sun-dried tomatoes, olives, garlic, lemon juice, and remaining olive oil for relish. Serve mackerel topped with relish.

Nutritional Facts (Per Serving): Calories: 380 | Carbs: 8g | Protein: 24g | Fat: 17g | Fiber: 8g | Sodium: 450mg | Sugars: 4g

Crispy Skillet Trout with Almond and Lemon Crust

Prep: 10 minutes | Cook: 15 minutes | Serves: 1

Ingredients:

- 1 small trout fillet, skin-on (150g)
- 1 tbsp whole grain flour (10g)
- 1 tbsp sliced almonds, crushed (10g)
- Zest of 1/2 lemon (1g)
- 1 tbsp olive oil (15ml)
- 1/4 tsp garlic powder (0.5g)
- 1/4 tsp sea salt (1.5g)
- 1/4 tsp black pepper (0.5g)

Instructions:

1. Combine whole grain flour, crushed almonds, lemon zest, garlic powder, salt, and pepper in a small bowl.
2. Pat the trout fillet dry and press the almond mixture onto the flesh side to form a crust.
3. Heat olive oil in a skillet over medium heat. Place the trout fillet skin-side down in the skillet and cook for 4-5 minutes until the skin is crisp.
4. Carefully flip the trout and cook the crusted side for 3-4 minutes, ensuring the almonds are golden but not burned, and the fish is cooked through.
5. Serve warm with a lemon wedge, if desired.

Nutritional Facts (Per Serving): Calories: 360 | Carbs: 5g | Protein: 24g | Fat: 17g | Fiber: 8g | Sodium: 450mg | Sugars: 1g

Moroccan Spiced Grilled Tuna Steaks with Harissa Yogurt

Prep: 10 minutes | Cook: 15 minutes | Serves: 1

Ingredients:

- 4 oz tuna steak (120g)
- 1/2 tsp ground cumin (1g)
- 1/4 tsp ground paprika (0.5g)
- 1/4 tsp ground coriander (0.5g)
- 1 tbsp olive oil, divided (15ml)
- 1 tbsp plain Greek yogurt (15g)
- 1/4 tsp harissa paste (1,5g)
- Juice of 1/2 lemon (15ml)
- 1/4 tsp sea salt (1.5g)
- 1/4 tsp black pepper (0.5g)

Instructions:

1. Mix cumin, paprika, coriander, salt, and pepper in a small bowl and rub onto the tuna steak.
2. Heat 1/2 tbsp olive oil in a grill pan over medium-high heat and sear the tuna for 2-3 minutes per side until cooked to your preference.
3. While the tuna cooks, whisk together the Greek yogurt, harissa paste, lemon juice, and remaining olive oil in a separate bowl until smooth.
4. Transfer the grilled tuna to a plate and let it rest for 1-2 minutes.

Nutritional Facts (Per Serving): Calories: 370 | Carbs: 6g | Protein: 25g | Fat: 16g | Fiber: 7g | Sodium: 480mg | Sugars: 2g

Basil and Pine Nut Crusted Baked Halibut

Prep: 10 minutes | Cook: 20 minutes | Serves: 1

Ingredients:

- 4 oz halibut fillet (120g)
- 1 tbsp fresh basil, chopped (5g)
- 1/2 tbsp (7g) pine nuts, crushed
- 1/2 tbsp (5g) whole grain flour
- 1 tbsp olive oil, divided (15ml)
- Juice of 1/2 lemon (15ml)
- 1/4 tsp sea salt (1.5g)
- 1/4 tsp black pepper (0.5g)

Instructions:

1. Preheat oven to 400°F (200°C).
2. In a small bowl, mix basil, crushed pine nuts, whole grain flour, 1/2 tbsp olive oil, and lemon juice to create the crust mixture.
3. Season the halibut fillet with salt and pepper, then press the crust mixture firmly onto the top of the fillet.
4. Place the halibut on a baking sheet lined with parchment paper, drizzle with remaining olive oil, and bake for 15-20 minutes until the fish is cooked through and the crust is golden.

Nutritional Facts (Per Serving): Calories: 370 | Carbs: 7g | Protein: 24g | Fat: 16g | Fiber: 8g | Sodium: 450mg | Sugars: 2g

Mediterranean Swordfish with Roasted Peppers and Capers

Prep: 10 minutes | Cook: 20 minutes | Serves: 1

Ingredients:

- 4 oz swordfish steak (120g)
- 1/2 cup roasted red peppers, sliced (75g)
- 1 tbsp capers (15g)
- 1 tbsp olive oil, divided (15ml)
- Juice of 1/2 lemon (15ml)
- 1 clove garlic, minced (3g)
- 1/4 tsp dried oregano (0.5g)
- 1/4 tsp sea salt (1.5g)
- 1/4 tsp black pepper (0.5g)

Instructions:

1. Heat 1/2 tbsp olive oil in a skillet over medium heat. Season swordfish with salt, pepper, and oregano, and sear for 4-5 minutes per side until cooked through.
2. In the same skillet, add garlic, roasted peppers, capers, lemon juice, and remaining olive oil, cooking for 2-3 minutes until warmed through.
3. Serve the swordfish topped with the pepper and caper mixture, garnished with a drizzle of the pan juices.

Nutritional Facts (Per Serving): Calories: 380 | Carbs: 9g | Protein: 23g | Fat: 17g | Fiber: 7g | Sodium: 480mg | Sugars: 3g

CHAPTER 17: DINNER: Festive Family Feasts: Dishes for Special Gatherings

One-Pan Chicken Marbella with Olives and Capers

Prep: 10 minutes | Cook: 20 minutes | Serves: 1

Ingredients:

- 4 oz boneless, skinless chicken thigh (120g)
- 1/4 cup pitted green olives, halved (30g)
- 1 tbsp capers (15g)
- 1 tbsp olive oil (15ml)
- 1 clove garlic, minced (3g)
- 1 tbsp red wine vinegar (15ml)
- 1/4 tsp dried oregano (0.5g)
- 1/4 tsp sea salt (1.5g)
- 1/4 tsp black pepper (0.5g)

Instructions:

1. Heat olive oil in a skillet, season and sear chicken for 4-5 minutes per side.
2. Add garlic, olives, capers, and red wine vinegar to the skillet, stirring to combine.
3. Reduce heat, cover, and simmer for 10 minutes until chicken is cooked through.

Nutritional Facts (Per Serving): Calories: 360 | Carbs: 8g | Protein: 24g | Fat: 16g | Fiber: 8g | Sodium: 500mg | Sugars: 3g

Slow-Braised Beef with Tomato and Red Wine Sauce

Prep: 10 minutes | Cook: 20 minutes | Serves: 1

Ingredients:

- 4 oz lean beef, cubed (120g)
- 1/2 cup diced tomatoes (100g)
- 1/4 cup red wine (60ml)
- 1 tbsp olive oil (15ml)
- 1 clove garlic, minced (3g)
- 1/4 tsp dried thyme (0.5g)
- 1/4 tsp sea salt (1.5g)
- 1/4 tsp black pepper (0.5g)

Instructions:

1. Heat olive oil in a skillet, sear beef for 4-5 minutes until browned.
2. Add garlic, thyme, salt, pepper, wine, and tomatoes.
3. Cover, simmer on low for 10-12 minutes until tender. Serve warm, garnished with thyme.

Nutritional Facts (Per Serving): Calories: 370 | Carbs: 10g | Protein: 23g | Fat: 17g | Fiber: 7g | Sodium: 480mg | Sugars: 4g

Tuscan White Bean and Sausage Stew with Fresh Thyme

Prep: 10 minutes | Cook: 20 minutes | Serves: 1

Ingredients:

- 4 oz Italian sausage, sliced (120g)
- 1/2 cup canned white beans, drained and rinsed (120g)
- 1/2 cup diced tomatoes (100g)
- 1 tbsp olive oil (15ml)
- 1 clove garlic, minced (3g)
- 1/2 cup chicken broth (120ml)
- 1 tsp fresh thyme, chopped (2g)
- 1/4 tsp sea salt (1.5g)
- 1/4 tsp black pepper (0.5g)

Instructions:

1. Heat olive oil in a skillet over medium heat. Sear sausage slices for 4-5 minutes until browned.
2. Add minced garlic to the skillet and sauté for 1 minute until fragrant, stirring frequently to avoid burning.
3. Stir in the white beans, diced tomatoes, chicken broth, thyme, salt, and pepper.
4. Simmer for 10-12 minutes until the flavors meld and the sauce thickens slightly.

Nutritional Facts (Per Serving): Calories: 370 | Carbs: 20g | Protein: 24g | Fat: 16g | Fiber: 8g | Sodium: 480mg | Sugars: 3g

Roasted Chicken with Sumac, Garlic, and Lemon Yogurt Sauce

Prep: 10 minutes | Cook: 20 minutes | Serves: 1

Ingredients:

- 4 oz chicken breast, skin-on (120g)
- 1 tsp sumac (2g)
- 1 tbsp olive oil (15ml)
- 1 clove garlic, minced (3g)
- 1/4 tsp sea salt (1.5g)
- 1/4 tsp black pepper (0.5g)
- 2 tbsp plain Greek yogurt (30g)
- Juice of 1/2 lemon (15ml)

Instructions:

1. Preheat oven to 400°F (200°C).
2. In a small bowl, mix olive oil, minced garlic, sumac, sea salt, and black pepper to form a seasoning paste.
3. Rub the seasoning paste all over the chicken breast, ensuring it is evenly coated on both sides.
4. Place the chicken breast skin-side up on the prepared baking sheet and roast in the oven for 18-20 minutes or until the skin is golden and the internal temperature reaches 165°F (74°C).
5. In a small bowl, mix yogurt with lemon juice to make the sauce.

Nutritional Facts (Per Serving): Calories: 360 | Carbs: 7g | Protein: 24g | Fat: 15g | Fiber: 7g | Sodium: 450mg | Sugars: 2g

Spiced Lamb Meatballs in Warm Tomato and Cinnamon Sauce

Prep: 10 minutes | Cook: 20 minutes | Serves: 1

Ingredients:

- 4 oz ground lamb (120g)
- 1/4 tsp ground cumin (0.5g)
- 1/4 tsp ground cinnamon (0.5g)
- 1 tbsp olive oil, divided (15ml)
- 1 tbsp whole grain flour (10g)
- 1/2 cup diced tomatoes (100g)
- 1 clove garlic, minced (3g)
- 1/4 tsp sea salt (1.5g)
- 1/4 tsp black pepper (0.5g)

Instructions:

1. In a bowl, mix ground lamb, cumin, cinnamon, whole grain flour, salt, and pepper. Shape into small meatballs.
2. Heat 1/2 tbsp olive oil in a skillet over medium heat, cook meatballs for 4-5 minutes, turning to brown all sides, then set aside.
3. In the same skillet, heat remaining olive oil, sauté garlic for 1 minute, then add diced tomatoes, cinnamon, and salt. Simmer for 5-6 minutes.
4. Return meatballs to the skillet and cook for another 5 minutes until fully cooked.

Nutritional Facts (Per Serving): Calories: 360 | Carbs: 10g | Protein: 23g | Fat: 16g | Fiber: 8g | Sodium: 450mg | Sugars: 4g

One-Pan Beef and Roasted Vegetable Bake with Herbs

Prep: 10 minutes | Cook: 20 minutes | Serves: 1

Ingredients:

- 4 oz lean ground beef (120g)
- 1 cup mixed vegetables, diced (e.g., zucchini, bell peppers, and eggplant) (150g)
- 1 tbsp olive oil (15ml)
- 1 tsp fresh rosemary, chopped (2g)
- 1 clove garlic, minced (3g)
- 1/4 tsp sea salt (1.5g)
- 1/4 tsp black pepper (0.5g)

Instructions:

1. Preheat oven to 400°F (200°C).
2. Toss diced vegetables with olive oil, garlic, rosemary, salt, and pepper, and spread evenly on a baking sheet.
3. Shape the ground beef into small patties or crumbles and place them among the vegetables.
4. Bake for 18-20 minutes, stirring halfway through, until the beef is cooked and the vegetables are tender and golden.
5. Serve warm, garnished with additional rosemary if desired.

Nutritional Facts (Per Serving): Calories: 370 | Carbs: 12g | Protein: 24g | Fat: 16g | Fiber: 8g | Sodium: 460mg | Sugars: 3g

CHAPTER 18: BONUSES

Effortless Mediterranean Meal Plans & Shopping Guides

This 30-day meal plan and grocery shopping lists make Mediterranean cooking simple and enjoyable. Focused on fresh, nutrient-rich ingredients, these plans support healthy eating and balanced nutrition. The shopping lists are designed for one person, ensuring you buy only what's needed—minimizing waste and streamlining meal prep. Enjoy effortless, flavorful meals with a well-structured approach to Mediterranean dining.

Shopping List for 7-Day Meal Plan

Meat & Poultry:

- **Boneless, skinless chicken breast** – 1 lb / 450 g (*Mediterranean One-Pan Balsamic Chicken, Chicken Marbella, Mediterranean Chicken and Eggplant Stew*)
- **Ground lamb** – ½ lb / 225 g (*One-Skillet Moroccan Lamb with Olives, Garlic and Herb Marinated Lamb Chops*)
- **Chicken thighs** – ½ lb / 225 g (*Chicken Marbella*)
- **Ground beef** – ½ lb / 225 g (*Garlic and Cumin-Spiced Beef with Sweet Potatoes*)
- **Turkey cutlets** – ½ lb / 225 g (*Balsamic Glazed Turkey Cutlets*)

Fish & Seafood:

- **Shrimp (large, peeled, deveined)** – ½ lb / 225 g (*Shrimp Saganaki*)
- **Trout fillet (skin-on)** – 1 small fillet (*Crispy Skillet Trout with Almond and Lemon Crust*)
- **Tuna steak** – 4 oz / 120 g (*Moroccan Spiced Grilled Tuna Steaks*)

Vegetables:

- **Eggplant** – 2 large (*Roasted Eggplant and Tahini Spread, Tomato and Eggplant Stew, Mediterranean Chicken and Eggplant Stew*)
- **Zucchini** – 1 medium (*Quinoa and Warm Chickpea Bowl, Bulgur and Roasted Zucchini Salad*)
- **Cherry tomatoes** – 2 cups / 300 g (*Shrimp Saganaki, Mediterranean One-Pan Balsamic Chicken*)
- **Red bell peppers** – 2 medium (*Frittata with Roasted Red Peppers and Mozzarella, Muhammara, Garlic and Herb Marinated Lamb Chops*)
- **Butternut squash** – ½ medium (*Wild Rice and Roasted Butternut Squash Bowl*)
- **Spinach (fresh)** – 2 bunches (*Scrambled Eggs with Smoked Salmon, Macaroni with Greek Yogurt and Spinach, Mediterranean Casserole*)
- **Kale** – 1 small bunch (*Hearty Farro and Vegetable Soup*)
- **Cucumber** – 1 large (*Labneh with Herbs, Cucumber and Mint Yogurt Salad*)
- **Onions (yellow or red)** – 2 medium (*Spanish Tortilla, Garlic and Cumin-Spiced Beef*)
- **Garlic** – 1 bulb (*Various dishes*)
- **Lemons** – 6 medium (*Mediterranean One-Pan Balsamic Chicken, Moroccan Spiced Tuna, One-Pan Chicken Marbella, Mediterranean Chicken and Eggplant Stew*)
- **Pomegranate seeds** – ½ cup / 75 g (*Pomegranate and Pistachio Ricotta Mousse, Labneh with Herbs*)
- **Fresh mint** – 1 small bunch (*Cucumber and Mint Yogurt Salad, Labneh with Herbs, Pomegranate Mousse*)
- **Fresh basil** – 1 small bunch (*Tomato and Eggplant Stew, Macaroni with Greek Yogurt and Spinach, Pomegranate Mousse*)

Fruits:

- **Figs (dried or fresh)** – 4 pieces (*Buckwheat Porridge with Walnuts and Figs, Baked Polenta with Figs and Walnuts*)
- **Dried cherries** – ¼ cup / 40 g (*Freekeh Breakfast Bowl with Dried Cherries*)
- **Blueberries** – 1 cup / 150 g (*Chia and Blueberry Power Smoothie*)
- **Oranges** – 2 large (*Pomegranate and Pistachio Ricotta Mousse, Moroccan Spiced Grilled Tuna Steaks*)
- **Bananas** – 1 medium (*Whole Wheat Banana and Honey Cake*)

Grains & Bread:

- **Buckwheat groats** – ½ cup

- / 90 g (*Buckwheat Porridge with Walnuts and Figs*)
- **Farro** – ½ cup / 90 g (*Hearty Farro and Vegetable Soup*)
- **Wild rice** – ½ cup / 90 g (*Wild Rice and Roasted Butternut Squash Bowl*)
- **Freekeh** – ½ cup / 90 g (*Freekeh Breakfast Bowl with Dried Cherries*)
- **Quinoa** – ½ cup / 90 g (*Quinoa and Warm Chickpea Bowl with Lemon Zest*)
- **Whole wheat macaroni** – ½ cup / 90 g (*Macaroni with Greek Yogurt, Spinach, and Dill*)
- **Whole wheat flour** – 1 cup / 150 g (*Pistachio and Lemon Buckwheat Pancakes, Mediterranean Olive Oil and Citrus Cake, Whole Wheat Banana and Honey Cake*)
- **Couscous** – ½ cup / 90 g (*Couscous and Warm Chickpea Bowl*)
- **Bulgur wheat** – ½ cup / 90 g (*Bulgur and Roasted Zucchini Salad*)

Dairy & Eggs:

- **Eggs** – 12 large (*Various recipes: Frittata, Scrambled Eggs, Baked Pancakes, Mediterranean Breakfast Pizza, Pancakes, Cakes*)
- **Greek yogurt (plain, full-fat)** – 2 cups / 500 g (*Labneh with Herbs, Cucumber and Mint Yogurt Salad, Pomegranate Mousse, Chia and Blueberry Power Smoothie, Cheesecake*)
- **Feta cheese** – 6 oz / 170 g (*One-Skillet Moroccan Lamb, Mediterranean Breakfast Pizza, Scrambled Eggs with Smoked Salmon, Tomato and Eggplant Stew*)
- **Mozzarella (fresh)** – 4 oz / 115 g (*Frittata with Roasted Red Peppers and Mozzarella, Tomato and Mozzarella Caprese*)
- **Ricotta cheese** – 4 oz / 115 g (*Ricotta and Honey Baked Pancakes, Pomegranate and Pistachio Ricotta Mousse*)

Nuts, Seeds & Nut Butter:

- **Walnuts** – ½ cup / 75 g (*Buckwheat Porridge with Walnuts and Figs, Baked Polenta with Figs and Walnuts, Mediterranean Apple Clafoutis*)
- **Pistachios (chopped or whole)** – ¼ cup / 40 g (*Pistachio and Lemon Buckwheat Pancakes, Pomegranate and Pistachio Ricotta Mousse*)
- **Almonds (whole or chopped)** – ¼ cup / 40 g (*Crispy Skillet Trout with Almond and Lemon Crust, Mediterranean Olive Oil and Citrus Cake*)
- **Tahini** – ¼ cup / 40 g (*Roasted Eggplant and Tahini Spread, Zaatar-Spiced Chickpea and Tahini Dip, Muhammara, Cheesecake*)
- **Sesame seeds** – ¼ cup / 40 g (*Tahini and Maple Syrup Brownies, No-Bake Chocolate and Olive Oil Tart with Sea Salt*)

Pantry Staples:

- **Olive oil (extra virgin)** – 1 bottle (*Various recipes*)
- **Balsamic vinegar** – 2 tbsp / 30 ml (*Mediterranean One-Pan Balsamic Chicken, Tomato and Mozzarella Caprese*)
- **Honey** – ¼ cup / 60 ml (*Ricotta and Honey Baked Pancakes, Cheesecake, Pomegranate Mousse, Banana Cake*)
- **Cinnamon** – 1 small jar (*Buckwheat Porridge, Whole Wheat Banana and Honey Cake, Apple Clafoutis*)
- **Cumin** – 1 small jar (*Garlic and Cumin-Spiced Beef, Moroccan Spiced Tuna, Mediterranean Chicken and Eggplant Stew*)
- **Paprika (sweet or smoked)** – 1 small jar (*One-Skillet Moroccan Lamb, Garlic and Herb Marinated Lamb Chops, Quinoa and Warm Chickpea Bowl*)
- **Sumac** – 1 small jar (*Cucumber and Mint Yogurt Salad, Garlic and Herb Marinated Lamb Chops*)
- **Dried oregano** – 1 small jar (*Shrimp Saganaki, Mediterranean One-Pan Balsamic Chicken, Chicken Marbella*)

Shopping List for 8-14 Day Meal Plan

Meat & Poultry:

- **Boneless, skinless chicken breast** – 1 lb / 450 g (*Moroccan Chicken with Green Olives, Roasted Chicken with Sumac and Lemon Yogurt*)
- **Ground lamb** – ½ lb / 225 g (*Spiced Lamb Meatballs with Tomato Sauce*)
- **Turkey cutlets** – ½ lb / 225 g (*Balsamic Glazed Turkey Cutlets*)
- **Beef (cubed, lean cut)** – ½ lb / 225 g (*Slow-Braised Beef with Tomato and Red Wine*)
- **Ground beef** – ½ lb / 225 g (*One-Pan Beef and Roasted Vegetable Bake*)

Fish & Seafood:

- **Mackerel fillets** – 6 oz / 170 g (*Roasted Mackerel with Olive and Tomato Relish*)
- **Swordfish steak** – 4 oz / 120 g (*Mediterranean Swordfish with Roasted Peppers*)

Vegetables:

- **Eggplant** – 1 large (*Baked Eggplant and Eggs with Sumac, Spaghetti with Sun-Dried Tomatoes and Basil Pesto*)
- **Zucchini** – 1 medium (*Zucchini and Chickpea Soup with Thyme, Tortellini with Roasted Peppers and Ricotta*)
- **Cherry tomatoes** – 2 cups / 300 g (*Egg and Ricotta Bake with Roasted Tomatoes, Roasted Mackerel with Olive and Tomato Relish, Spaghetti with Sun-Dried Tomatoes and Basil Pesto*)
- **Red bell peppers** – 2 medium (*Tortellini with Roasted Peppers and Ricotta, Spiced Lamb Meatballs with Tomato Sauce*)
- **Butternut squash** – ½ medium (*Pasta with Butternut Squash and Sage*)
- **Kale (Tuscan)** – 1 small bunch (*Tuscan Kale and Cannellini Bean Soup*)
- **Spinach (fresh)** – 1 bunch (*Spaghetti with Sun-Dried Tomatoes and Basil Pesto, Herb-Infused Omelet with Olives and Feta*)
- **Cucumber** – 1 medium (*Cucumber and Mint Cooler Smoothie*)
- **Onions (yellow or red)** – 2 medium (*Slow-Braised Beef with Tomato and Red Wine, One-Pan Beef and Roasted Vegetable Bake*)
- **Garlic** – 1 bulb (*Various dishes*)
- **Lemons** – 5 medium (*Roasted Chicken with Sumac and Lemon Yogurt, Mediterranean Swordfish with Roasted Peppers, Pasta with Butternut Squash and Sage*)
- **Olives (Kalamata or green)** – ½ cup / 75 g (*Herb-Infused Omelet with Olives and Feta, Moroccan Chicken with Green Olives, Roasted Mackerel with Olive and Tomato Relish*)
- **Fresh thyme** – 1 small bunch (*Zucchini and Chickpea Soup with Thyme, Pasta with Butternut Squash and Sage*)
- **Fresh rosemary** – 1 small bunch (*Balsamic Glazed Turkey Cutlets*)

Fruits:

- **Persimmons** – 2 large (*Cinnamon-Spiced Persimmons with Ricotta*)
- **Figs (dried or fresh)** – 4 pieces (*Rosewater and Fig Chia Pudding with Almonds*)
- **Blueberries** – ½ cup / 75 g (*Cucumber and Mint Cooler Smoothie*)
- **Oranges** – 2 large (*Orange and Almond Mediterranean Muffins*)
- **Bananas** – 1 medium (*Whole Wheat Banana and Honey Cake*)
- **Apricots (dried)** – ¼ cup / 40 g (*Almond and Apricot Bars*)

Grains & Bread:

- **Spelt flakes** – ½ cup / 90 g (*Spelt Breakfast Bowl with Hazelnuts and Chocolate*)
- **Whole wheat spaghetti** – ½ cup / 90 g (*Spaghetti with Sun-Dried Tomatoes and Basil Pesto*)
- **Whole wheat pasta (any shape)** – ½ cup / 90 g (*Pasta with Butternut Squash and Sage, Tortellini with Roasted Peppers and Ricotta*)
- **Whole wheat flour** – 1 cup / 150 g (*Orange and Almond Mediterranean Muffins, Whole Wheat Banana and Honey Cake, No-Bake Chocolate and Olive Oil Tart*)
- **Chia seeds** – ¼ cup / 40 g (*Rosewater and Fig Chia Pudding with Almonds*)

Dairy & Eggs:

- **Eggs** – 12 large (*Egg and Ricotta Bake with Roasted Tomatoes, Herb-Infused Omelet with Olives and Feta, Various Pancakes & Cakes*)
- **Ricotta cheese** – 6 oz / 170 g (*Egg and Ricotta Bake with Roasted Tomatoes, Tortellini with Roasted Peppers and Ricotta, Cinnamon-Spiced Persimmons with Ricotta*)
- **Feta cheese** – 6 oz / 170 g (*Herb-Infused Omelet with Olives and Feta, Spaghetti with Sun-Dried Tomatoes and Basil Pesto*)
- **Parmesan cheese** – 4 oz / 115 g (*Italian Tomato and Basil Soup with Parmesan, Pasta with Butternut Squash and Sage*)
- **Almond milk (unsweetened)** – 1 cup / 240 ml (*Rosewater and Fig Chia Pudding with Almonds*)
- **Greek yogurt (plain, full-fat)** – 1 cup / 250 g (*Cucumber and Mint Cooler Smoothie*)

Nuts, Seeds & Nut Butter:

- **Hazelnuts (whole or chopped)** – ½ cup / 75 g (*Spelt Breakfast Bowl with Hazelnuts and Chocolate, Hazelnut and Cocoa Nib Cookies*)
- **Almonds (whole or chopped)** – ¼ cup / 40 g (*Rosewater and Fig Chia Pudding with Almonds, Almond and Apricot Bars*)
- **Walnuts** – ¼ cup / 40 g (*No-Bake Chocolate and Olive Oil Tart*)
- **Sesame seeds** – ¼ cup / 40 g (*Tahini and Dark Chocolate Truffles*)
- **Cocoa nibs** – ¼ cup / 40 g

(*Hazelnut and Cocoa Nib Cookies*)
- **Dark chocolate (85% cocoa or higher)** – ½ cup / 75 g (*Tahini and Dark Chocolate Truffles, No-Bake Chocolate and Olive Oil Tart*)

Pantry Staples:

- **Olive oil (extra virgin)** – 1 bottle (*Various recipes*)
- **Balsamic vinegar** – 2 tbsp / 30 ml (*Balsamic Glazed Turkey Cutlets, Spaghetti with Sun-Dried Tomatoes and Basil Pesto*)
- **Tahini** – ¼ cup / 40 g (*Tahini and Dark Chocolate Truffles*)
- **Honey** – ¼ cup / 60 ml (*Cinnamon-Spiced Persimmons with Ricotta, No-Bake Chocolate and Olive Oil Tart, Whole Wheat Banana and Honey Cake*)
- **Cinnamon** – 1 small jar (*Cinnamon-Spiced Persimmons with Ricotta, Whole Wheat Banana and Honey Cake*)
- **Cumin** – 1 small jar (*Spiced Lamb Meatballs with Tomato Sauce, Moroccan Chicken with Green Olives*)
- **Paprika (sweet or smoked)** – 1 small jar (*Balsamic Glazed Turkey Cutlets, Moroccan Chicken with Green Olives*)
- **Sumac** – 1 small jar (*Baked Eggplant and Eggs with Sumac, Roasted Chicken with Sumac and Lemon Yogurt*)
- **Dried oregano** – 1 small jar (*Shrimp Saganaki, Mediterranean Swordfish with Roasted Peppers, Moroccan Chicken with Green Olives*)

Shopping List for 15-21 Day Meal Plan

Meat & Poultry:

- **Boneless, skinless turkey cutlets** – ½ lb / 225 g (*Balsamic Glazed Turkey Cutlets*)
- **Italian sausage (mild or spicy)** – ½ lb / 225 g (*Tuscan White Bean and Sausage Stew*)
- **Ground lamb** – ½ lb / 225 g (*Warm Farro and Grilled Lamb Salad*)
- **Boneless, skinless chicken breast** – 1 lb / 450 g (*Mediterranean Chicken with Artichokes, One-Pan Mediterranean Chicken with Capers, One-Pan Chicken Marbella with Olives*)
- **Ground beef** – ½ lb / 225 g (*Garlic and Cumin-Spiced Beef*)

Fish & Seafood:

- No seafood required for this meal plan.

Vegetables:

- **Zucchini** – 2 medium (*Zucchini and Feta Breakfast Frittata, Chickpea and Zucchini Stew*)
- **Red bell peppers** – 2 medium (*Muhammara, Roasted Red Pepper and Yogurt Dip*)
- **Cherry tomatoes** – 1 cup / 150 g (*Savory Chickpea Flour Pancakes with Tomatoes*)
- **Artichoke hearts (jarred or canned)** – ½ cup / 75 g (*Mediterranean Chicken with Artichokes*)
- **Spinach (fresh)** – 1 small bunch (*Buckwheat and Spinach Bowl*)
- **Kale (Tuscan)** – 1 small bunch (*Chickpea and Zucchini Stew with Fresh Mint*)
- **Cauliflower** – ½ medium head (*Millet and Roasted Cauliflower Bowl*)
- **Potatoes (yellow or red-skinned)** – 2 medium (*Spanish Tortilla with Potatoes and Onions*)
- **Onions (yellow or red)** – 2 medium (*Spanish Tortilla with Potatoes and Onions, Tomato and Basil One-Pan Turkey with Lentils*)
- **Garlic** – 1 bulb (*Various recipes*)
- **Lemons** – 5 medium (*Lemon and Olive Oil Detox Smoothie, Balsamic Glazed Turkey Cutlets, One-Pan Chicken Marbella with Olives*)
- **Olives (Kalamata or green)** – ½ cup / 75 g (*One-Pan Chicken Marbella with Olives, Zaatar-Spiced Chickpea and Tahini Dip*)
- **Fresh mint** – 1 small bunch (*Chickpea and Zucchini Stew with Fresh Mint, Lemon and Olive Oil Detox Smoothie*)
- **Fresh basil** – 1 small bunch (*Tomato and Basil One-Pan Turkey with Lentils*)
- **Fresh thyme** – 1 small bunch (*One-Pan Chicken Marbella with Olives*)
- **Fresh rosemary** – 1 small bunch (*Balsamic Glazed Turkey Cutlets*)

Fruits:

- **Strawberries** – ½ cup / 75 g (*Polenta Breakfast Bowl with Ricotta and Strawberries*)
- **Pomegranate seeds** – ¼ cup / 40 g (*Pomegranate and Pistachio Ricotta Mousse*)
- **Oranges** – 2 large (*Orange and Almond Mediterranean Muffins*)
- **Apples (red or green)** – 1 large (*Couscous Bowl with Almond Butter and Apples*)
- **Raisins** – ¼ cup / 40 g (*Raisin*

and Walnut Greek Easter Cookies)

Grains & Bread:

- **Buckwheat groats** – ½ cup / 90 g (*Buckwheat and Spinach Bowl*)
- **Freekeh (cracked wheat)** – ½ cup / 90 g (*Freekeh and Roasted Mushrooms Bowl*)
- **Millet** – ½ cup / 90 g (*Millet and Roasted Cauliflower Bowl*)
- **Farro (whole grain or pearled)** – ½ cup / 90 g (*Warm Farro and Grilled Lamb Salad*)
- **Whole wheat farfalle pasta** – ½ cup / 90 g (*Farfalle with Peas and Mint*)
- **Whole wheat couscous** – ½ cup / 90 g (*Couscous Bowl with Almond Butter and Apples*)
- **Whole wheat flour** – 1 cup / 150 g (*Greek Yogurt and Olive Oil Cake, Orange and Almond Mediterranean Muffins, No-Bake Chocolate and Olive Oil Tart*)

Dairy & Eggs:

- **Eggs** – 12 large (*Zucchini and Feta Breakfast Frittata, Spanish Tortilla with Potatoes and Onions, Raisin and Walnut Greek Easter Cookies*)
- **Ricotta cheese** – 6 oz / 170 g (*Polenta Breakfast Bowl with Ricotta and Strawberries, Pomegranate and Pistachio Ricotta Mousse*)
- **Feta cheese** – 6 oz / 170 g (*Zucchini and Feta Breakfast Frittata, Herb-Infused Omelet with Olives and Feta*)
- **Greek yogurt (plain, full-fat)** – 1 cup / 250 g (*Greek Yogurt and Olive Oil Cake, Roasted Red Pepper and Yogurt Dip*)
- **Parmesan cheese** – 4 oz / 115 g (*Farfalle with Peas and Mint*)

Nuts, Seeds & Nut Butter:

- **Almonds (whole or chopped)** – ½ cup / 75 g (*Orange and Almond Mediterranean Muffins, Couscous Bowl with Almond Butter and Apples, No-Bake Chocolate and Olive Oil Tart*)
- **Walnuts** – ½ cup / 75 g (*Raisin and Walnut Greek Easter Cookies*)
- **Pistachios (whole or chopped)** – ¼ cup / 40 g (*Pomegranate and Pistachio Ricotta Mousse*)
- **Sesame seeds** – ¼ cup / 40 g (*Zaatar-Spiced Chickpea and Tahini Dip*)
- **Tahini (sesame paste)** – ¼ cup / 40 g (*Zaatar-Spiced Chickpea and Tahini Dip, Muhammara*)
- **Almond butter** – ¼ cup / 40 g (*Couscous Bowl with Almond Butter and Apples*)
- **Dark chocolate (85% cocoa or higher)** – ½ cup / 75 g (*No-Bake Chocolate and Olive Oil Tart*)

Pantry Staples:

- **Olive oil (extra virgin)** – 1 bottle (*Various recipes*)
- **Balsamic vinegar** – 2 tbsp / 30 ml (*Balsamic Glazed Turkey Cutlets, Warm Farro and Grilled Lamb Salad*)
- **Honey** – ¼ cup / 60 ml (*Greek Yogurt and Olive Oil Cake, No-Bake Chocolate and Olive Oil Tart, Orange and Almond Mediterranean Muffins*)
- **Cinnamon** – 1 small jar (*Raisin and Walnut Greek Easter Cookies, Couscous Bowl with Almond Butter and Apples*)
- **Cumin** – 1 small jar (*Muhammara, Tomato and Basil One-Pan Turkey with Lentils*)
- **Paprika (sweet or smoked)** – 1 small jar (*Muhammara, Roasted Red Pepper and Yogurt Dip*)
- **Sumac** – 1 small jar (*Zaatar-Spiced Chickpea and Tahini Dip, One-Pan Mediterranean Chicken with Capers*)
- **Dried oregano** – 1 small jar (*Tomato and Basil One-Pan Turkey with Lentils, One-Pan Chicken Marbella with Olives*)

Shopping List for 22-28 Day Meal Plan

Meat & Poultry:

- ***Boneless, skinless chicken breast*** – 1 ½ lbs / 680 g (*One-Pan Chicken with Mushrooms, Greek-Style Grilled Chicken with Lemon Yogurt, Chicken with Artichokes and Capers, Roasted Chicken with Sumac and Yogurt Sauce*)
- ***Ground turkey*** – ½ lb / 225 g (*Mediterranean Turkey Meatballs*)
- ***Ground beef*** – ½ lb / 225 g (*Spiced Ground Beef with Pine Nuts*)
- ***Beef stew meat (cubed, lean cut)*** – 1 lb / 450 g (*Tomato and Garlic Beef Stew with Basil, Slow-Braised Beef with Tomato and Red Wine*)
- ***Lamb shoulder (bone-in or boneless, trimmed)*** – ½ lb / 225 g (*Moroccan Spiced Lamb Shoulder*)

Fish & Seafood:

- ***Tuna steaks*** – 6 oz / 170 g (*Grilled Tuna Steaks with*

Harissa Yogurt)
- **Halibut fillet** – 6 oz / 170 g (Basil and Pine Nut Crusted Halibut)
- **Swordfish steak** – 6 oz / 170 g (Mediterranean Swordfish with Roasted Peppers)

Vegetables:

- **Mushrooms (cremini or white button)** – 1 cup / 150 g (One-Pan Chicken with Mushrooms)
- **Spinach (fresh)** – 1 bunch (Spinach and Ricotta Quiche with Pine Nuts)
- **Cherry tomatoes** – 1 cup / 150 g (Tomato and Basil Bruschetta with Poached Eggs)
- **Tomatoes (large, ripe)** – 2 medium (Tomato and Basil Bruschetta with Poached Eggs, Tomato and Garlic Beef Stew with Basil)
- **Bell peppers (red or yellow)** – 2 medium (Roasted Red Pepper and Yogurt Dip, Mediterranean Swordfish with Roasted Peppers)
- **Eggplant** – 1 medium (Slow-Braised Beef with Tomato and Red Wine)
- **Artichoke hearts (jarred or canned)** – ½ cup / 75 g (Chicken with Artichokes and Capers)
- **Garlic** – 1 bulb (Various recipes)
- **Lemons** – 5 medium (Greek-Style Grilled Chicken with Lemon Yogurt, Basil and Pine Nut Crusted Halibut, Mediterranean Swordfish with Roasted Peppers, Roasted Chicken with Sumac and Yogurt Sauce)
- **Olives (Kalamata or green)** – ½ cup / 75 g (Mediterranean Breakfast Pizza with Feta)
- **Pomegranate seeds** – ¼ cup / 40 g (Labneh with Fresh Herbs and Pomegranate, Pomegranate and Pistachio Ricotta Mousse)
- **Fresh basil** – 1 small bunch (Tomato and Basil Bruschetta with Poached Eggs)
- **Fresh thyme** – 1 small bunch (Slow-Braised Beef with Tomato and Red Wine)
- **Fresh parsley** – 1 small bunch (Greek-Style Grilled Chicken with Lemon Yogurt, Mediterranean Turkey Meatballs)
- **Fresh mint** – 1 small bunch (Labneh with Fresh Herbs and Pomegranate, Pomegranate and Pistachio Ricotta Mousse)

Fruits:

- **Figs (fresh or dried)** – 4 pieces (Baked Polenta with Figs and Walnuts)
- **Pomegranates (or seeds pre-packed)** – ¼ cup / 40 g (Labneh with Fresh Herbs and Pomegranate, Pomegranate and Pistachio Ricotta Mousse)
- **Apricots (dried, unsweetened)** – ¼ cup / 40 g (Almond and Apricot Bars)
- **Oranges** – 1 large (Saffron and Almond Milk Panna Cotta)
- **Pistachios (unsalted, whole or chopped)** – ¼ cup / 40 g (Pistachio and Lemon Buckwheat Pancakes)
- **Lemon zest** – 1 tsp (Pistachio and Lemon Buckwheat Pancakes)

Grains & Bread:

- **Buckwheat flour** – ½ cup / 75 g (Pistachio and Lemon Buckwheat Pancakes)
- **Whole wheat flour** – 1 cup / 150 g (Savory Herb and Cheese Scones, Almond and Apricot Bars, Tahini and Maple Syrup Brownies, No-Bake Chocolate and Olive Oil Tart)
- **Whole wheat pasta (spaghetti or other shape)** – ½ cup / 90 g (One-Pan Chicken with Mushrooms)
- **Polenta (coarse ground)** – ½ cup / 90 g (Baked Polenta with Figs and Walnuts)
- **Brown rice** – ½ cup / 90 g (Brown Rice Pudding with Coconut Milk)

Dairy & Eggs:

- **Eggs** – 12 large (Mediterranean Breakfast Pizza with Feta, Spinach and Ricotta Quiche with Pine Nuts, Tomato and Basil Bruschetta with Poached Eggs)
- **Feta cheese** – 6 oz / 170 g (Mediterranean Breakfast Pizza with Feta, Spinach and Ricotta Quiche with Pine Nuts)
- **Ricotta cheese** – 6 oz / 170 g (Pomegranate and Pistachio Ricotta Mousse)
- **Greek yogurt (plain, full-fat)** – 1 cup / 250 g (Roasted Red Pepper and Yogurt Dip, Roasted Chicken with Sumac and Yogurt Sauce)
- **Parmesan cheese** – 4 oz / 115 g (Spinach and Ricotta Quiche with Pine Nuts, One-Pan Chicken with Mushrooms)
- **Mascarpone** – 4 oz / 115 g (Saffron and Almond Milk Panna Cotta)

Nuts, Seeds & Nut Butter:

- **Almonds (whole or chopped)** – ½ cup / 75 g (Saffron and Almond Milk Panna Cotta, Almond and Apricot Bars, No-Bake Chocolate and Olive Oil Tart)
- **Walnuts** – ½ cup / 75 g (Baked Polenta with Figs and

Walnuts)
- **Pistachios (whole or chopped)** – ¼ cup / 40 g (Pistachio and Lemon Buckwheat Pancakes, Pomegranate and Pistachio Ricotta Mousse)
- **Pine nuts** – ¼ cup / 40 g (Spinach and Ricotta Quiche with Pine Nuts, Basil and Pine Nut Crusted Halibut)
- **Tahini (sesame paste)** – ¼ cup / 40 g (Tahini and Maple Syrup Brownies)

Pantry Staples:

- **Olive oil (extra virgin)** – 1 bottle (Various recipes)
- **Balsamic vinegar** – 2 tbsp / 30 ml (Grilled Tuna Steaks with Harissa Yogurt, Basil and Pine Nut Crusted Halibut)
- **Coconut milk (canned, unsweetened)** – ½ cup / 120 ml (Brown Rice Pudding with Coconut Milk)
- **Honey** – ¼ cup / 60 ml (Pomegranate and Pistachio Ricotta Mousse, No-Bake Chocolate and Olive Oil Tart)
- **Maple syrup (pure, no additives)** – ¼ cup / 60 ml (Tahini and Maple Syrup Brownies)
- **Cinnamon** – 1 small jar (Brown Rice Pudding with Coconut Milk, Almond and Apricot Bars)
- **Cumin** – 1 small jar (Spiced Ground Beef with Pine Nuts)
- **Paprika (sweet or smoked)** – 1 small jar (Roasted Red Pepper and Yogurt Dip)
- **Sumac** – 1 small jar (Roasted Chicken with Sumac and Yogurt Sauce)
- **Harissa paste** – 2 tbsp / 30 ml (Grilled Tuna Steaks with Harissa Yogurt)